AFTA SpringerBriefs in Family Therapy

A Publication of the American Family Therapy Academy

Founded in 1977, the **American Family Therapy Academy** is a non-profit organization of leading family therapy teachers, clinicians, program directors, policymakers, researchers, and social scientists dedicated to advancing systemic thinking and practices for families in their social context.

Vision

AFTA envisions a just world by transforming social contexts that promote health, safety, and well-being of all families and communities.

Mission

AFTA's mission is developing, researching, teaching, and disseminating progressive, just family therapy and family-centered practices and policies.

More information about this series at http://www.springer.com/series/11846

Karen Mui-Teng Quek · Shi-Ruei Sherry Fang
Editors

Transition and Change in Collectivist Family Life

Strategies for Clinical Practice with Asian Americans

AFTA
American Family Therapy Academy

Springer

Editors
Karen Mui-Teng Quek
Marital & Family Therapy and Mental Health Counseling Programs
Bethel Seminary, Bethel University
San Diego, CA
USA

Shi-Ruei Sherry Fang
Human Development and Family Sciences, Family and Child Studies
Northern Illinois University
DeKalb, IL
USA

ISSN 2196-5528 ISSN 2196-5536 (electronic)
AFTA SpringerBriefs in Family Therapy
ISBN 978-3-319-50677-7 ISBN 978-3-319-50679-1 (eBook)
DOI 10.1007/978-3-319-50679-1

Library of Congress Control Number: 2017933852

Printed on acid-free paper

This Springer imprint is published by Springer Nature
The registered company is Springer International Publishing AG
The registered company address is: Gewerbestrasse 11, 6330 Cham, Switzerland

Series Editor Foreword

The *AFTA SpringerBriefs in Family Therapy* is an official publication of the American Family Therapy Academy. Each volume focuses on the practice and policy implications of innovative systemic research and theory in family therapy and allied fields. Our goal is to make information about families and systemic practices in societal contexts widely accessible in a reader-friendly, conversational, and practical style. AFTA's core commitment to equality, social responsibility, and justice is represented in each volume.

In *Transition and Change in Collectivist Family Life: Strategies for Clinical Practice with Asian Americans*, Karen Mui-Teng Quek and Shi-Ruei Sherry Fang have put together a collection of articles designed to bridge research and contextually informed practice. In contrast to approaches that broadly stereotype Asian clientele or are informed primarily by first-generation experience, this book explores the nuances and tensions involved as Asian American families grapple with change. Each chapter offers an inside look at relational units such as husband and wife, daughter-in-law and mother-in-law, grandparents and their adult children as they confront work and family choices, changes in roles and hierarchies, parenting, and spiritual/religious values and communities. Their research examines how family members manage societal contexts such as patriarchy and class while also bringing to light changing (and not changing) meanings around intergenerational and bonds and loyalties and couple dynamics.

Quek and Fang resist the impulse to generalize Asian American families and instead offer a sample of the diversity within this large umbrella classification. As a researcher, I recognize the commitment and dedication necessary to do this kind of intimate study. As a clinician and family therapy educator, I value the details and examples provided—and admit to being surprised by some of the findings. The cultural lens applied to this research helps readers interpret family patterns and cultural dilemmas that could easily be misunderstood and pathologized or overlooked all together. Each author offers suggestions to guide clinical practice and expand therapists' understandings of the kind of services that might be helpful. Readers will find themselves enriched by the strengths and commitments of the Asian American families profiled in this interesting book.

Carmen Knudson-Martin
Series Editor
AFTA SpringerBriefs in Family Therapy
Lewis & Clark College
Portland, OR, USA

Acknowledgments

This collection of essays is a scholarly contribution that addresses contemporary issues encountered by Asian Americans with respect to familial relationships, multiple roles, gender, social hierarchy, and domestic violence. Increasingly aware of the cultural, historical, and experiential differences among Asian Americans, the groups represented in this collection are Chinese, Koreans, Filipinos, Taiwanese, and Southeast Asian Americans from Cambodia, Laos, Myanmar, and Vietnam. Latest research findings in each chapter reflect one aspect of their relational journeys in the United States.

The authors featured in this collection come from different places in Asia: Singapore, Thailand, Taiwan, Korea, and the United States of America. Most of us arrived here for higher education but are now in the United States of America and identify ourselves as Asian Americans. The authors each base their work on their personal interest in the narratives of Asian Americans and attempt to shed light on how perspectives about each subgroup differ depending on their life stages and experiences.

As far as possible we have organized the analysis of Asian American families across the life span reflecting on how individuals embody the culture they come from and negotiating the differences that arise in the course of day-to-day interaction. These essays remind us again and again of how complex relational and social contexts continue to be: gender issues are intertwined with cultural norms, cultural norms are intertwined with personal narratives, and personal narratives are always both gendered and cultural. Navigating this balance continues to be one of America's deepest needs as America becomes more racially and culturally diverse. We are grateful for the countless respondents who willingly participated and shared their stories.

Great connections help us bring this project to fruition. For this success, we wish to express our heartfelt thanks to Dr. Carmen Knudson-Martin, editor for this series, for her invitation to contribute and her tremendous support as we put this book together. A big thank you to Natalie Kwan, writer, attorney, and nonprofit development professional, for providing valuable feedback on the manuscripts. We are grateful to the American Family Therapy Academy for promoting the importance of multi-voiced scholarship and for sponsoring the AFTA SpringerBriefs in Family Therapy that makes it possible for us to share our work with a wider audience. Thank you Jennifer Hadley and the team at Springer for overseeing this project every step of the way. Many thanks to all chapter authors who work tirelessly in reviewing and resubmitting their work in order to make their content more readable for a wider audience. Thank you for engaging in this important work.

Karen Mui-Teng Quek, Ph.D., LMFT, LPCC
Shi-Ruei Sherry Fang, Ph.D.

Contents

1 **How Asian-American Couples Create Relational Harmony: Collectivism and Gender Equality** 1
Karen Mui-Teng Quek and Carmen Knudson-Martin

2 **Addressing Power and Resistance with Chinese American Daughters-in-Law and Their Immigrant Mothers-in-Law** 11
Kristy Y. Shih

3 **Through Religion: Working-Class Korean Immigrant Women Negotiate Patriarchy** 21
Seongeun Kim

4 **Bridging the Relational Space Between First- and Second-Generation Chinese American Christians** 33
Jessica ChenFeng

5 **From Walking the Thin Line Between Work and Family to Self-compassion: Working with Asian American Career Mothers** 45
Kandice Hsu and Liang-Ying Chou

6 **The Role of Chinese Grandparents in Their Adult Children's Parenting Practices in the United States** 57
Hao-Min Chen and Denise C. Lewis

7 **Balancing the Old and the New: The Case of Second-Generation Filipino American Women** 67
Jennifer L. Del-Mundo and Karen Mui-Teng Quek

8 Cultural Transmission to Cultural Transformation: The Case of Contemporary Chinese Americans in a Faith-Based Community 79
Peter C. Lim

9 Bicultural Identity as a Protective Factor Among Southeast Asian American Youth Who Have Witnessed Domestic Violence 89
Skultip (Jill) Sirikantraporn

Editors and Contributors

About the Editors

Karen Mui-Teng Quek, Ph.D., LMFT, LPCC is currently Associate Professor and Program Director of Marital & Family Therapy and Mental Health Counseling programs at Bethel Seminary, Bethel University, San Diego, CA. Her research interest is in the study of familial and dyadic relationships which examine the interplay of various diversity constructs in the context of evolving societal changes. Karen has contributed substantially to academic literature on relational changes associated with gender, martial power, and multiculturalism.

Shi-Ruei Sherry Fang, Ph.D. is Professor in the School of Family and Consumer Sciences at Northern Illinois University. Her research mainly focuses on ethnic families and children, effects of poverty on children, parent–child interaction, and immigrant families and children. Sherry has published extensively on issues related to social justices, family dynamics, and parent–child relationships in immigrant families.

Contributors

Hao-Min Chen Couple and Family Therapy Program, Alliant International University, Irvine, CA, USA

Jessica ChenFeng Department of Educational Psychology and Counseling, California State University, Northridge, CA, USA

Liang-Ying Chou Private Practice, Los Angeles, CA, USA

Jennifer L. Del-Mundo Private Practice, Irvine, CA, USA

Kandice Hsu Orange County Health Care Agency, Santa Ana, CA, USA

Seongeun Kim Sungkyunkwan University, Seoul, South Korea

Carmen Knudson-Martin Counseling Psychology Department, Lewis and Clark College, Portland, OR, USA

Denise C. Lewis College of Family and Consumer Sciences, University of Georgia, Athens, GA, USA

Peter C. Lim Ambassador NetWork, Brea, CA, USA

Karen Mui-Teng Quek Marital & Family Therapy and Mental Health Counseling Programs, Bethel Seminary, Bethel University, San Diego, CA, USA

Kristy Y. Shih Human Development and Family Studies, Central Michigan University, Mount Pleasant, MI, USA

Skultip (Jill) Sirikantraporn California School of Professional Psychology, Alliant International University, San Diego, CA, USA

Chapter 1
How Asian-American Couples Create Relational Harmony: Collectivism and Gender Equality

Karen Mui-Teng Quek and Carmen Knudson-Martin

Social harmony is valued in collectivism (Hsiung and Ferrans 2007). Independent behaviors or emotional expressions that might disrupt harmony are discouraged. But Chinese Americans live in a multicultural context. Besides embracing collectivist values, Chinese American women and men actively participate in the dominant culture that celebrates values such as individual rights, personal autonomy, and self-determination (Kibria 2002; Kim et al. 2014; Osyerman et al. 2002). In this chapter, we (Karen and Carmen) examine the ways Chinese American couples with young children utilize these contrasting sets of values to negotiate family life.

Karen is a Chinese Singaporean who teaches in a couple and family therapy program in the U.S. She has invested many years studying relational dynamics between individuals in couples from Singapore, America, Greece, China, and the Philippines. Carmen is a woman of Euro–American heritage who directs a marriage, couple, and family therapy program. She has a special interest on how gender, culture, and power impact couple relationships. In our previous work together, we found that couples in Singapore seem to maintain aspects of both collectivism and individualism as they move toward more equal partnerships (Quek and Knudson-Martin 2006, 2008; Quek et al. 2011). We are intrigued by how Chinese American couples in the U.S. manage these issues.

This chapter is a revised version of Quek, K., Knudson-Martin, C., Rue, D., & Alabiso, C. (2010). Relational harmony: A new model of collectivism and gender equality among Chinese American couples. *Journal of Family Issues, 31*, 358–380.

K.M.-T. Quek (✉)
Marital & Family Therapy and Mental Health Counseling Programs,
Bethel Seminary, Bethel University, San Diego, CA, USA
e-mail: karen-quek@bethel.edu

C. Knudson-Martin
Counseling Psychology Department, Lewis and Clark College, Portland, OR, USA

K.M.-T. Quek and S.-R.S. Fang (eds.), *Transition and Change in Collectivist Family Life*, AFTA SpringerBriefs in Family Therapy,
DOI 10.1007/978-3-319-50679-1_1

Social Harmony, Self-directedness, and Equality

We approach this study from a social constructionist perspective in which relationship patterns are seen as ongoing phenomena, constructed and reconstructed through daily interactions (Gergen 2009). Although marital interaction is highly influenced by the options available within a given societal context, we believe that partners also have the potential to create and modify how they perform gender and culture in their lives. As such, elements of social harmony and self-directedness are likely to be in flux.

To maintain traditional social harmony, individuals interact in prescribed ways that minimize direct conflict and social discord (Hsiung and Ferrans 2007). Communication flows downward from superior to subordinate, and roles are informed by family membership, social position, gender, age, and social status rather than qualification and ability. Therefore, the husband performs as head of the household but still shows deference and loyalty to his father and older brothers. The wife–mother acts as the relational link between her husband and children and typically defers to her husband for major and public decisions. Social sensitivity and other-directedness are vital to maintaining social harmony (Glicken 2006).

Self-directedness tends to be valued in the Euro–American cultural context and reportedly contributes to life satisfaction (Kwan et al. 1997). Self-directed persons rely on their own judgment in choosing a course of action. They value expression of one's opinions, thinking for oneself, self-reliance, and achievement of one's goals (Hofstede 2001). Persons who strongly endorse self-directedness typically hold less traditional attitudes toward marital roles than those who value social harmony (Triandis 1995).

We consider equality in terms of partners' relative status in the relationship and the extent to which each accommodates and attends to the other (e.g., Knudson-Martin and Mahoney 2009). We expect that in equal relationships, partners are mutually able to influence the other and that relationship patterns and decisions reflect the interests, opinions, and needs of both partners. These egalitarian ideals are widespread across Western societies (Sullivan 2006); however, taken-for-granted gender patterns tend to organize family life such that equality is still often more a myth or aspiration than a reality (Coontz 2005; Knudson-Martin and Mahoney 2009).

Method

In order to explore how Asian-American couples in the U.S. draw on collectivist and individualistic values, and how gender hierarchies are transformed or maintained in this process, we interviewed 20 heterosexual Asian-American couples with young children. Interviews focused on how they established parenting, family, and household responsibilities and how they attended to and communicated with each other. Questions were open-ended so that participants could expand on issues most meaningful to them. The analysis followed the techniques for developing grounded theory (Corbin and Strauss 2008; Quek et al. 2010).

Harmony: A Unifying Concept

All the couples in the study appeared to prioritize harmony. However, they did so in different ways. Three couples endorsed a relatively traditional form of harmony that emphasized social norms and order, which we termed "structural harmony." Nine couples practiced a new "relational harmony" that integrated values from both individualism and collectivism and emphasized mutuality within the marriage. Eight fell on the spectrum in between these two forms of harmony. To examine how these families fashion harmony, let us look inside a few homes. In the examples that follow, we illustrate the distinctions between relational harmony and structural harmony, with an emphasis on how they relate to gender equality.

Structural Harmony

Structural harmony is based on social norms that support obligation to the whole. Couples in this category retained traditional collectivist patterns even if wives worked outside the home. Their relationships include: (1) a focus on order, (2) hierarchical authority structure, (3) rigid roles, (4) one voice, and (5) norm directed behavior. Taken together, these elements maintain a hierarchical and gendered relationship system.

Dawn and Dave: A model for structural harmony. Dave and Dawn live in a middle class neighborhood. They are proud parents of three boys, 9-year-old James, 7-year-old Jessie, and 5-year-old Jack. Dave is an educator. When their firstborn arrived, it was a taken-for-granted that Dawn would give up her paid position in a corporation and assume the role of a full-time homemaker.

Order. Dawn, like the other couples classified as Structural Harmony, said that smooth functioning was more important than equality or fairness: "When you think about being fair or desiring equality … it just creates more problems." She later emphasized that in their home, she and Dave seek to carry out their "roles and responsibilities." She retains structural order by asking, "What role am I supposed to take to make it a better relationship?" In response to her own question, she remarks,

> My responsibility is to be a supportive wife for Dave. Hopefully there's not too much stress at home when he comes home … I'll be able to have dinner on the table so that he doesn't have to worry about what's for dinner … and oh … like the household chores, I guess things that I need to call for carpet cleaning or trying to fix appliances if something is broken.

Hierarchical. Dave recognizes that Dawn's role is difficult and is aware that as a male and the sole provider, he could continue to do the same things that he normally did when their child was born:

> For example, between last year and this year after our firstborn arrived, I wouldn't change as far as my job responsibilities and the time I spend … Sometimes if I just want to go out, it's easier for me to go out. I didn't really adjust too much in what I do, but obviously Dawn has had to change a lot.

Though Dave helped with bathing and feeding whenever he was home because it made Dawn happy, Dawn is the primary parent in the family and Dave fits parenting around his work life.

Structural harmony ties decision-making to family roles and position. Male headship creates order by giving the husband authority to decide; however, Dave may elect to defer power to his wife when it comes to issues concerning their children. Though she describes internal struggles, Dawn accepts her role in order to maintain peace. This upholds a gendered hierarchy wherein men are privileged over women.

Rigid roles. Cultural gender norms guide Dawn's explanation of her role: "The fact that I'm female and because I'm a mother … so I think of myself … [in] the role of caregiver." She orchestrates Dave's involvement with their son: "Dave comes home and gets to play with the baby and have daddy time while I make dinner." Dave is not expected to be knowledgeable about children: "I would ask, 'What do I do now [with my son]? He is in his ninth month' … and I yell at her when she doesn't know … because she is supposed to know everything and she can fix it all."

One voice. In order to avoid unpleasant interaction, one voice represents the dyad at any one time. If there are two perspectives, both women and men may hold back to avoid conflict. But Dawn and Dave are very clear on whose voice is primary. For example, when asked about how the couple makes decisions, Dawn remarked, "Before I schedule anything I always check with Dave to hear what he says … I defer to him because he's in charge of all of that in our household and in a way that's his power." Though Dawn has the "expert voice" in childrearing, Dave is consulted for final decisions within this household.

Norm directed. Dave and Dawn dutifully model their relationship roles according to what they believe is expected and modeled by Dave's immigrant parents. The couple did not see any choice in how they structured their roles. However, Dave recognizes that as a male he has somewhat more personal freedom than she does:

> She has to stay at home and take care of Aaron when I'm more flexible in what I can do … I can kind of hang out and talk to coworkers or go out spur of the moment to do a couple more things and then come home.

He is aware that she misses "'me' time and time with other people without having to worry about having someone at [her] side all the time." However, the couple does not see a different option for family organization.

Couples who describe living primarily within structural harmony see limited choices in how to organize their lives. When partners organize their lives according to cultural norms, personal sacrifices for the common good are expected and are not always acknowledged. Though this applies to men as well as women, in a structural harmony paradigm, women seemed to carry an especially heavy burden for keeping the family going smoothly, and opportunities for mutuality between the partners appear limited.

Relational Harmony

Relational harmony assumes and promotes equal partnership. These couples creatively synthesize their collectivist roots with individualistic values of the dominant culture to construct this type of harmony. It includes (1) a focus on mutuality, (2) a collaborative authority structure, (3) flexible roles, (4) two voices, and (5) personal agency. Taken together, these elements create a more egalitarian relationship system.

Kristy and James: A model for relational harmony. Relational harmony appears focused on maximizing mutuality. Even though the relationship remains primary over individual needs, individual expression is encouraged and personal desires are acknowledged. Kristy and James are a dual-career couple with two children—Jamie, 9 years old and Jenny, 4 years old. Kristy is a physician and John works as an educator. As they continue to struggle, negotiate, and recreate a relationship that mutually benefits both, they are aware that there is nothing automatic about their model for relational harmony. They have to work out all the details.

Mutuality. When a couple values relational harmony, their marital commitment shifts from an obligation to the institution of marriage to a commitment between partners. The relationship is characterized by mutual respect for each other and for each other's desires and needs. Kristy elaborated by suggesting that mutuality embraces differences of opinions: "Even though two people can be completely different, whatever they say and do would have some merits" and therefore is worthy of serious consideration. In contrast to Western models that emphasize male autonomy (e.g., Jordan 2004; Knudson-Martin and Mahoney 1999), both women and men appear attuned to the needs of the relationship and their partner's needs. Partners think in terms of "we" rather than "you" or "I." James indicates that mutuality includes an expectation of equality whereby "two people still nurture each other" as the milieu of family life continues to change. With the arrival of their firstborn, both of them struggled with frustration and ambivalence produced by the competing demand of paid work and parent care. Kristy recalls, "I did talk about James staying home to watch Jamie and I would work full time because financially that would make more sense. But he wants to work and I think it's good for him to work." James adds, "Both of us have made sacrifices in our work schedules and personal time when we have Jamie."

Collaborative. Relational harmony is based on a collaborative authority structure that shares responsibility for decision-making. These partners describe "having equal say," "making deals," collecting and evaluating information together, and accepting the other's point of view. Couples describe a shared effort to decide what is best for their family. As young parents to Jamie, Kristy and James express different priorities for their daughter. Kristy worries about the details in Jamie's life. Is she clean? Is she well-fed? James asks, "Is she happy?" But both fully participate in the decision-making and neither feels entitled to "always get what they want." Acknowledging that communication with Kristy is essential regarding all aspects of childcare, James takes an active role in identifying the daily routines that center around "who's picking her up, who's dropping her off." Collaboratively they recognize "that we really need to make sure we are on the same page … We want to avoid confusion for her because she's not old enough to know that we both have different toleration levels."

Flexible roles. In relational harmony, couples demonstrate role flexibility. Both husbands and wives feel free to modify their roles within the family structure as needed, rather than determine them by gender or tradition. Work and family tasks are negotiated according to availability, choice, and family needs. Even though Kristy and James have established a routine flow of their everyday lives whereby Kristy takes Jamie to daycare every day because James' workplace is much farther from home, he brings their daughter home two days a week. During the summer, James is off from teaching, so he has more time to take care of the children in order for Kristy to continue her level of commitment at work.

Men are clear that they share responsibility for household and childcare tasks. James shares what he believes to be their practices: "We don't really have assigned tasks. If something bothers you more, you do it." To support his statement, Kristy chimes in, "What I noticed was a lot of stuff to do at home. I end up putting my energy to taking care of the baby, and washing bottles for her … But then I'll leave our dishes alone and then after a while, James will get irritated and he'll wash ours." James adds, "Washing dishes is simple for me and I take care of the rest … Since I don't have the baby, it's easier for me to get food for our dinner. Also whoever is at home makes sure Jamie gets fed."

Two voices. Relational harmony intentionally includes multiple perspectives. Kristy states that she usually has interesting conversations with James because "he likes to ask questions where there's probably no right or wrong answers." He sees this as important to maintaining harmony. James has his own opinion on certain issues, but he wants to know "my opinion. I could be sitting there thinking hard because nobody has ever asked me before." So for Kristy, this relationship allows her the opportunity to get her point across, the opportunity to show what's bothering her, even if her voice and perspective could be different than James'.

Self-directed. Relational harmony recognizes individual experience and choice. As emphasized by James, Kristy is very verbal. Therefore, she has no qualms about expressing her personal goals, and James supports her choices just as much as she supports his. Both of them want to work, but the decision to work has different meaning to each of them. To her, it makes good financial sense for her to work full time, while to him, he sees his work as essential to his sense of being. In relational harmony, both partners consider their own wants and desires, as well as those of the partner; both feel free to take initiative and vocalize their desires, and these are processed within the couple's construct of "we." To maintain relational harmony, couples appear to deliberately not privilege male goals and interests.

In-between structural and relational harmony: Couples in transition. Although we are able to categorize couples to facilitate understanding of the processes involved in structural and relational harmony, most couples, to varying degrees, move back and forth between them. The structural harmony mindset is still well ingrained. Accordingly, a couple's move toward relational harmony does not simply happen. Many experience a push-and-pull process in which they learn to balance the multiple influences in their lives. At least 30% of the couples interviewed show the most evidence of being in the transitional phase. These couples describe tensions along each of the dimensions that contribute to structural or relational harmony: (1) conflict between relational and structural goals; (2) unclear authority structure; (3) intersection of family and workplace; (4) harmonizing multiple voices; and (5) incorporating personal agency.

Competencies for Counseling Asian-American Couples: Collectivism, Individualism, and Harmony

Therapists should be aware that Asian-Americans are likely to value harmony but may be in some kind of transition regarding how it is practiced. Many contemporary Asian-American couple relationships have challenged the traditional social order and have modified and transformed the marital system. They have forged a pattern that is highly "we" focused, but also more equal than traditional gender structures. They are creating a new type of harmony that embraces individualistic values such as collaborative decision-making, flexible roles, two voices, self-directedness and validation of partners. While family is still the central value, priority is given to caring for the marital dyad and the nuclear family. Therapists working with Chinese American couples must therefore enter into a continual process of understanding the experiences of the couple before them instead of adhering to preconceived assumptions about collectivism among this ethnic group.

First, couple therapists need to assess the varying facets of harmony that Asian-American couples exhibit. Though many 1.5- and second-generation Asian-Americans are changing the meaning of social harmony, it is critical to know the type of harmony—structural harmony, relational harmony, and the in-betweens—that informs their relationship. Figure 1.1 provides a useful guide.

Secondly, couple therapists need to focus on the gender context. For many Asian-Americans, the pull between multicultural worlds with differing gender practices remains a struggle. Most couples are likely to find that their values and actual practices may sometimes contradict. How to manage ambiguities in gender hierarchies and an equitable division of work and family labor may leave some couples confused about appropriate roles and what is fair. Dealing with the conflict

RELATIONAL HARMONY HARMONY IS THE RESULT OF THE RELATIONSHIP BETWEEN PARTNERS.		STRUCTURAL HARMONY HARMONY IS THE RESULT OF A SET OF ROLES AND RULES
Mutuality. Shared commitment toward maintaining the relationship.	*Goal* *Issue: What is the purpose of attaining harmony?*	**Order.** Regulate behavior to fit within taken-for-granted societal norms.
Collaborative. Decisions are expected to be shared. Even when husband is framed as the head of the family, he is not assumed to have the authority to make decisions alone.	*Authority Structure* *Issue: How is power shared in the decision-making process?*	**Hierarchical.** Decision-making authority is tied to role and position in the family. Male head has ultimate authority, but may elect to defer power to wife.
Flexible roles. Work and family tasks negotiated according to availability, choice, and family needs.	*Division of labor* *Issue: How is the intersection of family and workplace managed?*	**Rigid roles.** Work and family tasks assumed on the basis of cultural rules regarding gender.
Two voices. Harmony intentionally includes multiple perspectives.	*Expression of Differences* *Issue: How are multiple voices harmonized?*	**One voice.** Harmony requires aligning with the perspective of dominant partner or family elders.
Self-directed. Individual recognized as source of his or her own experience and choice.	*Personal agency* *Issue: How is free will integrated into the marriage?*	**Norm directed.** Personal experience and options determined by cultural roles and rules.

Fig. 1.1 Social harmony assessment guide. Adapted from Quek et al. (2010)

arising from giving voice to multiple perspectives may also be a challenge, and women in particular may feel guilty as they attempt to harmonize personal agency with the needs of the family as a whole.

Therapists should help couples unravel the multiple strands of social expectations rooted in gender dynamics, and encourage considering and fostering shared responsibility for monitoring family welfare and mutual concerns for professional development. There have been successful stories of Asian-American couples who learn to engage both the collectivist norm of “we-ness” and the individualistic value of self-directedness (Quek et al. 2010). In fact, we found that the collectivist focus has helped men engage more willingly in shared responsibility for the relationship and household tasks.

Thirdly, couple therapists could attune to gender-specific issues based on collectivist values and traditions. It is not uncommon for Asian-American wives to hold quite closely to the notion of male headship. Wives who express this view most often do not want to forego mutuality and shared decision-making but still want their husbands to fulfill a leadership role. It is also not uncommon for Asian-American men to restrain emotion, as traditional collectivist values foster the restriction of male emotion for the sake of upholding the family name and preserving one’s reputation. The Asian-American men in this study seemed to want an equal partnership with their wives and expected to take on household tasks. We encourage therapists to identify and validate these positive shifts and help both women and men reframe masculine ideals such that they are functioning more adaptively and flexibly with a far richer range of behavioral and emotional skills.

Finally, couple therapists must attend to the ambivalence of cultural modification experienced by those couples vacillating between relational and structural goals and obligations, unclear authority structures, the intersection of family and workplace, conflict when two voices are expressed, and incorporating personal agency for both women and men. Conscious negotiation of these issues is likely to make more options visible to couples and help them devise a satisfying cultural integration. These couples will also benefit from education that helps them successfully bridge cultures in ways that work for them.

The relational orientation of collectivist cultures can help promote mutuality if therapists validate these cultural strengths and help couples, especially men, tap into them. Examples of questions for couples to explore are: How are mutuality and empathy experienced in your relationship? How has paying attention to your partner's personal and professional welfare enriched your sense of couple-hood and family?

References

Coontz, S. (2005). *Marriage, a history: From obedience to intimacy or how love conquered marriage*. New York: Viking.

Corbin, J., & Strauss, A. (2008). *Basics of qualitative research: Techniques and procedures for developing grounded theory* (3rd ed.). Thousand Oaks, CA: Sage.

Gergen, K. (2009). *An invitation to social construction* (2nd ed.). Newbury Park, CA: Sage.

Glicken, D. M. (2006). *Social work in the 21st century*. Thousand Oaks, CA: Sage.

Hofstede, G. (2001). *Culture's consequences*. Newbury Park, CA: Sage.

Hsiung, Y. Y., & Ferrans, E. C. (2007). Recognizing Chinese Americans' cultural needs in making end-of-life treatment decisions. *Journal of Hospice and Palliative Nursing, 9,* 132–140.

Jordan, J. (2004). Toward competence and connection. In J. V. Jordan, M. Walker, & L. M. Hartling (Eds.), *The complexity of connection* (pp. 111–127). New York, NY: Guilford.

Kibria, N. (2002). *Becoming Asian American*. London: The Johns Hopkins University Press.

Kim, L., Tuttle, A., & Knudson-Martin, C. (2014). Toward relationship-directed parenting: An example of North American born second generation Korean-American mothers and their partners. *Family Process, 53,* 55–66.

Knudson-Martin, C., & Mahoney, A. (1999). Beyond different worlds: A "postgender" approach to relational development. *Family Process, 38,* 325–340.

Knudson-Martin, C., & Mahoney, A. (Eds.). (2009). *Couples, gender, and power: Creating change in intimate relationships*. New York, NY: Springer Publishing.

Kwan, V., Bond, M., & Singleis, T. (1997). Pancultural explanations for life satisfaction: Adding relationship harmony to self-esteem. *Journal of Personality and Social Psychology, 73,* 1038–1051.

Osyerman, D., Coon, H. M., & Kemmelmeier, M. (2002). Rethinking individualism and collectivism: Evaluation of theoretical assumptions and meta-analyses. *Psychological Bulletin, 128,* 3–72.

Quek, K., & Knudson-Martin, C. (2006). A push toward equality: Processes among dual career newlywed couples in a collectivist culture. *Journal of Marriage and Family, 65,* 56–69.

Quek, K., & Knudson-Martin, C. (2008). Shifting marital equality: Qualitative analysis of collectivist couples. *Journal of Social and Interpersonal Relationship, 25,* 513–534.

Quek, K., Knudson-Martin, C., Orpen, S., & Victor, J. (2011). Gender equality in the transition to parenthood: A qualitative longitudinal analysis of dual-earner couples in Singapore. *Journal of Social and Personal Relationships*. doi:10.1177/0265407510397989.

Quek, K., Knudson-Martin, C., Rue, D., & Alabiso, C. (2010). Relational harmony: A new model of collectivism and gender equality among asian american couples. *Journal of Family Issues (Special Edition on Asian American Families), 31,* 358–380.

Sullivan, O. (2006). *Changing gender relations, changing families: Tracing the pace of change over time*. New York, NY: Rowman & Littlefield.

Triandis, H. (1995). *Individualism and collectivism*. Boulder, CO: Westview Press.

Chapter 2
Addressing Power and Resistance with Chinese American Daughters-in-Law and Their Immigrant Mothers-in-Law

Kristy Y. Shih

Contentious mother-/daughter-in-law relations have long been a popular soap opera theme. These in-law relations are also stereotyped as conflictual in the folklore and popular cultures of Asia and in the United States, and are often the subject of jokes, situation comedies, and movies (e.g., Everybody Loves Raymond, 1996–2005; Monster-in-law, 2005). The stereotype depicts the relationship between mothers- and daughters-in-law as fraught with jealousy and competition as these women vie for the affection and loyalty of the man who is the son to one and husband to the other. Their disagreements often center on how domestic tasks and childcare should be done, and who has the authority to make decisions (Shih and Pyke 2010). The man who is son to one and husband to the other is often depicted as being stuck in the middle trying to please two demanding, unreasonable women. Rarely are these women portrayed as unified in struggles against male family members and patriarchal arrangements. In fact, their conflicts are often trivialized, making it easier to poke fun at them. Despite the explicit sexism of such images and the rise of feminist scholarship over the past 40 years, there is still little scholarly literature on the dynamics between women of different generations who are thrown together through heterosexual marriage.

Research on in-law relationships has been sporadic. The lack of research on this important family relationship prompts several scholars to advocate for the need for such examination in family scholarship (see, Goetting 1990; Lee et al. 2003; Walker 2000). Recent research efforts have focused on the caregiver roles of

---

This chapter is a revised version of Shih, K. Y., & Pyke, K. (2010). Power, resistance, and emotional economies in women's relationships with mothers-in-law in Chinese immigrant families. *Journal of Family Issues, 31(3)*, 333–357.

K.Y. Shih (✉)
Human Development and Family Studies, Central Michigan University, Mount Pleasant, MI, USA
e-mail: shih1k@cmich.edu

K.M.-T. Quek and S.-R.S. Fang (eds.), *Transition and Change in Collectivist Family Life*, AFTA SpringerBriefs in Family Therapy,
DOI 10.1007/978-3-319-50679-1_2

daughters- and sons-in-law (e.g., Globerman 1996) and aid and support given to aging parents and parents-in-law (e.g., Lee et al. 2003; Shuey and Hardy 2003). Others have examined the influence of in-laws on marriage (Bryan et al. 2001) and relationship ambivalence (Turner et al. 2006; Wilson et al. 2003). Even when there is research on in-law relationships, most have studied white samples of mothers- and daughters-in-law, and seldom has research examined this relationship in families of a different racial/ethnic background (see, for exceptions, Jackson and Berg-Cross 1988; Shih and Pyke 2010; 2015).

There are several reasons that may contribute to such limited research on this type of family relationship. First, most family scholars focus their inquiry on primary family relationships, such as marital relations or parent–child relations; few place an emphasis on secondary family relationships, such as those between in-laws (Cotterill 1994; Turner et al. 2006; see also, Lopata 1999 for a discussion). Second, in-law relationships are multifaceted as they are often influenced and mediated by other relations in the family system (Turner et al. 2006). Finally, the complexity and sensitive nature of the mother- and daughter-in-law relationship make it difficult to find appropriate methods to study this relationship (Cotterill 1994; Turner et al. 2006). In this chapter, I examine gender and power dynamics of mother-in-law and daughter-in-law relationships in immigrant families from China, Hong Kong, and Taiwan.

I am a Taiwanese American sociologist who teaches in a Human Development and Family Studies program in the U.S. I have interests in, and have conducted research on, immigrant and transnational families, gendered family power dynamics, and intergenerational relationships. I have invested many years studying the power dynamics and relationships between mothers-in-law and daughters-in-law in Chinese, Taiwanese, and Mexican American families.

Understanding Hidden Power and Emotional Economies

In studying power relations, I consider overt as well as covert dynamics (Komter 1989; Lukes 1974). Overt power measures decision-making and conflict outcomes and assumes power is exercised in a direct and observable manner (Blood and Wolfe 1960). However, it does not address how power dynamics shape latent and invisible processes that prevent issues and conflicts from erupting to the surface (Komter 1989). One way covert power works is by preventing issues from being raised. This occurs when the less powerful individual anticipates the needs of the more powerful party and does not raise issues due to fear of a negative reaction. The less powerful individual, in choosing his/her actions, then internalizes the needs and desires of the more powerful person, even when doing so may compromise her/his own wishes. Because individuals are often unaware of covert power, it is important to assess whether respondents feel they can raise issues without fear of dire consequences, or if they desire changes that they do not attempt to implement because of a sense of helplessness.

I also draw on the concept of an emotional economy of entitlement, obligation, and gratitude (Hochschild 1989). Cultural ideologies concerning what certain family members owe to or are owed by other memberships inform emotional economies. For example, norms of filial piety can shape emotional interplays of entitlement and obligation and, in the process, also shape power dynamics between family members (Pyke 1999; Shih and Pyke 2010). Norms of filial piety can lead a mother-in-law to feel entitled to deference and service from her daughter-in-law, who might feel obligated to provide such care, thus reducing her power. In families that do not subscribe to filial piety, however, the mother-in-law will not feel entitled to such services and the daughter-in-law will not feel obligated to provide them. If the daughter-in-law provides caregiving services to her mother-in-law, those services are likely to be regarded as a gift for which the mother-in-law is expected to be grateful and is obligated to reciprocate in some way. However, mothers-in-law and daughters-in-law may not be in agreement about what constitutes a gift, what constitutes an obligation, what they owe, and what they are owed in their relationship. Conflicts, resentment, and resistance can occur when they disagree.

Method

Fifteen second-generation Chinese American daughters-in-law were interviewed about their relationships with their mothers-in-law. Each respondent is married to a Chinese American man whose mother is, like the respondent's own mother, a first-generation immigrant from China, Hong Kong, or Taiwan. Interviews focused on daughters-in-law's general feelings toward their mothers-in-law, conflicts, any shared interests or leisure activities, traits they like and dislike about them, domestic tasks they do together or provide for each other, expectations they have for their relationships, and instances when their mothers-in-law have tried to influence their home lives or marriages. Open-ended interview questions allowed interviewees to elaborate on their responses. Data are analyzed with a constant-comparative method and followed the strategies for developing grounded theory (Glaser 1965).

Domestic Expertise and Childrearing as Domains of Power, Gratitude, and Ambivalence

Most Chinese American women interviewed describe having mothers-in-law who display some degree of entitlement to the authority and deference accorded elders in traditional Chinese culture. Daughters-in-law typically feel obligated to show respect and honor toward their mothers-in-law. However, they do not feel they owe the older women unconditional or unearned deference.

Many Chinese immigrant mothers-in-law have to work at acquiring and maintaining their power by assuming the role of domestic "expert" to establish a hierarchal relationship with their daughters-in-law. They offer advice and recommendations to their daughters-in-law on matters of health, daily household management, meal preparation, finances, and childrearing.

Whether the mother-in-law is successful in her efforts to acquire and maintain power depends on if the daughter-in-law is grateful for her mother-in-law's advice or resents it as a threat, insult, or attempt to dominate. When a daughter-in-law is grateful, she is more likely to view such advice or assistance as a gift and follow her mother-in-law's wishes. Anne provides an example of a grateful daughter-in-law. Anne happily receives her mother-in-law's instructions and serves as her "helper" when they cook together. Anne says, "It's neat to be able to learn a few things that I didn't know and I'm appreciative that she is willing to teach me." In contrast, when daughters-in-law do not feel like they need the assistance or advice, they express resentment rather than gratitude toward the household services their mothers-in-law provided. Daughters-in-law interpret such advice or assistance as their mothers-in-law's lack of confidence in their ability to care for their families. Samantha says,

> If I'm cooking a Chinese dish and I forgot [to use] ginger, it's no big deal to me. [She'd say], "Oh, when I make that dish, I put ginger in it." I translate that to mean, "You think I'm cooking this wrong." I'm sure [that's what she means].

Madison shares another instance:

> When my husband and I first got married, my mother-in-law used to come over and she would bring two weeks' worth of food. It was kind of insulting to me because I felt like she was suggesting I wasn't feeding her son properly … She would also do laundry … I told my husband, "She doesn't have to do that. I know how to do laundry!"

Chinese American women who describe their mothers-in-law's advice as unwelcome believe they are using the guise of offering suggestions to give orders and criticize the way they manage their households and perform domestic tasks. These daughters-in-law perceive such advice as a burden imposed on them by their mothers-in-law. Many are offended by the implicit message that they are not good wives or mothers. In these relationships, the mother-in-law often has difficulty establishing power and authority in her interaction with her daughter-in-law because the younger woman does not feel obligated nor willing to defer to her demands. In addition, a daughter-in-law's resentment for having endured the burden of the mother-in-law's offensive intrusion can result in her feeling that something is owed to her in the emotional economy of their relationship.

Several women who resent their mothers-in-law for giving domestic and childrearing advice are limited in their resistance. This is partly due to their dependence on the assistance they receive from their mothers-in-law, for which they are grateful. They feel contradictory pulls of gratitude for those services and resentment toward their mothers-in-law's influence in their home lives. Their feelings of ambivalence often result in vacillation between resistance and deference to their mothers-in-law. Childcare is an area in which such ambivalence is the most evident. Ella provides the best example:

> I was trying to take my son off the bottles … I wanted everybody who was taking care of him to not feed him from the bottle, but try to feed him from the cup. My mother-in-law initially resisted. Every time we came home, we would find her picking up the bottle and feeding him.

As Ella explains, her feelings of gratitude and indebtedness to her mother-in-law make her unwilling and unable to impose her wishes:

> I thought I couldn't say anything because she was here taking care of my son while I was working. [I] felt like I owed her for that … I think about times [when] I get frustrated and I don't want to hurt her feelings. I sometimes feel bad [getting into conflicts with her] because she's helping out so much. I don't want to do anything that might make her feel like she's not wanted or her help is not appreciated.

Mia also experiences a lot of conflicts with her mother-in-law with regard to how to care for her infant son:

> When I had my first son, we left my son with her. We had certain things that we wanted her to do … [be]cause we were paranoid about SIDS. She wouldn't do it so that would upset me because I felt like I can't trust her … If she believes that we're not doing the right thing with our kids, she would overrule us … It made me feel annoyed because I feel like we're the parents, so parents should be the ones ultimately in charge of how we raise our kids.

Despite their conflicts, Mia is grateful to her mother-in-law for her childcare assistance. Mia's gratitude leads her to feel obligated to reciprocate, which she does by offering insincere praise to her mother-in-law. Mia continues, "I try to thank [her] for everything because that really goes a long way with her … I'll make a special effort to thank her for everything she does, however minor it is, so she won't feel unappreciated."

Chinese American women's reliance on their mothers-in-law's childcare assistance reduces their power. Although these women describe not liking the interference of their mothers-in-law, neither can they live without it. They thus move between resentment and gratitude, generating an emotional wave of ambivalence that stalls their resistance.

Husbands as Mediators

On their own, Chinese American daughters-in-law who depend on mothers-in-law's childcare assistance lack the power to bring their mothers-in-law into compliance. These wives turn to their husbands to negotiate on their behalves with their mothers-in-law when conflict or disagreement erupts. In most instances, their husbands tend to support their wives' resistance and do not insist that they implement their mothers' directives or behave as docile daughters-in-law. Husbands and wives thus enjoy a cross-gender alliance that empowers and elevates the status of daughters-in-law. In some situations, it is only after the husband joins his wife in reprimanding his mother that the older woman begins to change her behavior.

Mia frequently butts heads with her mother-in-law regarding childrearing issues until her husband steps in. She said of their childcare situation, "So finally my husband spoke to her and said, 'If you continue this way, we can't leave our son with you at all.' Then she started to do what we asked." Mia is confident that she enjoys greater power as a result of her husband's support: "My husband's pretty much on my side and [my mother-in-law] knows it, so she tries very hard to maintain a good relationship with me because she knows that she's going to be on the losing end."

Melissa's mother-in-law ignores her request that she stop carrying her baby daughter every time she cries until Melissa's husband mediates the situation. She says,

> My mother-in-law came out first to help out when my daughter was born. As soon as the baby made the slightest whimper, my mother-in-law would scoop her up … Her way of comforting the child was to walk her around the house and rock the baby in her arms to get her to stop crying … I said to her, "Mom, please stop carrying her around because I won't be able to do that when you leave." She kind of ignored me … Finally, my husband backed me up and told his mom, "Mom, you can't carry her around because when you leave, [Melissa's] not going to be able to handle carrying both of them just because one of them is crying …" My mother-in-law wasn't happy, but she stopped carrying my daughter around.

Chinese American daughters-in-law express that they would especially like their husbands to step into mediate in situations in which they feel they do not have the power to negotiate with or demand desired changes from their mothers-in-law. Daughters-in-law sometimes resent their husbands when they perceive their husbands to be unwilling to mediate conflicts, however. Pauline wants her husband to speak up and be firm with his mother, especially when the mother-in-law crosses the line with their children. It frustrates Pauline when she feels that her husband does not speak up enough on behalf of the kids. Pauline provides an example of when her mother-in-law was not getting along with and was being extremely critical of her oldest daughter:

> I was torn between [whether or not to] step in. I felt like as a parent, I needed to protect my daughter, but at the same time, I was afraid if I step in, my mother-in-law was going to see me as interfering or protecting her … So I was afraid I was going to make it worse for my daughter by my stepping in. I wanted my husband to do it. I felt like he wasn't doing it. I was getting frustrated with him. I said, "You need to stop the way your mother goes over the boundary with [our daughter]. You have to protect her; you are her parent!"

Pauline's story reveals her powerlessness. She worries about the possible repercussions both for herself and her daughter if she were to speak up against her mother-in-law. Pauline does not confront her mother-in-law due to her fear of her mother-in-law's negative reaction. However, she is torn as she needs to defend her daughter from her mother-in-law's criticism. There is no observable conflict between Pauline and her mother-in-law because conflicts are being suppressed. Conflicts would be observable if Pauline expressed her desires or voiced her concerns to her mother-in-law. In this situation, Pauline believes that only when her husband intervenes would her mother-in-law stop her criticism of their daughter.

Some daughters-in-law believe that it is not their place to question their mothers-in-law. They believe that their husbands are in a better place and have more power vis-à-vis their mothers to request changes. This perception could explain why many of the women in this study rely on their husbands to facilitate their relationships with their mothers-in-law. Emma puts it:

> If I really want to get a point across, I will just let my husband say it because he is better at being completely honest. I have to care about her feelings, but he doesn't. He has the leverage of being the son, and she will take whatever he says. She will argue with him, but at least it is her son … My husband can do whatever he wants because he is the son.

Most of the wives with children depend on the power and authority of their husbands to get their mothers-in-law to follow their wishes. Chinese American daughters-in-law in these families can elevate their power by bargaining with patriarchy. They draw on traditional male authority by enlisting their husbands' support and mediation as a strategy to maximize their power vis-à-vis their mothers-in-law. By so doing, they remain dependent on their husbands to represent their interests, and thus implicitly consent to and reproduce male authority.

The Covert "Backstage" Resistance of Daughters-in-Law

Chinese American daughters-in-law frequently engage a covert form of resistance by appearing to agree and comply with their mothers-in-law while not actually implementing their suggestions in their absence. They thus engage a formal or symbolic display of deference to their mothers-in-law in their presence. Ella feigns agreement with her mother-in-law's suggestions when in her presence, even when Ella does not agree with her advice. She nods her head in apparent agreement; however, she does not always carry out the advice when her mother-in-law is not around:

> With my son, if [my mother-in-law] tells me, "Morning is very cold and you have to keep him in pajamas for a little longer," most of the time she's not here in the morning, so I change him anyway. I don't keep him in his pajamas.

Stella explains her behavior when she does not agree with her mother-in-law:

> She talked and I listened and nodded, which is *typical* of most intergenerational interaction with your elder … There's supposed to be a way around that, which is you thank them for their advice and say, "I'll think about it." Just don't say no to their face.

Sarah refers to this kind of performance as a balancing act:

> I hear what you are saying. I may not necessarily do it, but I don't necessarily have to tell her that I didn't do it her way. Or I usually just say, "Okay, we've already taken care of it …" in a respectful way. Like saying, "I appreciate what you're saying, but we may not

> necessarily following what you are asking us …" It's kind of like balancing a fine act between not being obedient in a sense, and still being respectful.

Mia describes a similar performance in her interactions with her mother-in-law:

> She'll see something on TV or read something in the Chinese newspaper then she tries to tell me, "Don't do that or you shouldn't eat that." I just smile. In this way, I do the *Chinese thing*. I just smile and nod. But I totally ignore her [advice].

Mia explains that pretending to agree with her mother-in-law allows her to "keep peace" while also abiding traditional expectations of respect.

It is on the front stage that daughters-in-law are most likely to behave and interact in accordance with the norms, moral codes, and hierarchies associated with the cultural expectations of their immigrant parents-in-law. In the ethnic world of their mothers-in-law, Chinese American women display the filial respect and obedience that they understand is expected of "good" Chinese daughters-in-law by nodding, smiling, or saying nothing when they disagree. Further, by not overtly disagreeing, Chinese American daughters-in-law avoid open conflict without actually having to comply and give up power over their households. Even those daughters-in-law who are not dependent on the services of their mothers-in-law typically do not engage overt resistance for fear of hurting their feelings, showing disrespect, and creating the impression of being a "bad" daughter-in-law.

When they are on the backstage where their mothers-in-law are not present, however, Chinese American daughters-in-law have greater freedom and can enact values and norms that conflict with those that they appear to accept on the front stage. The backstage autonomy of daughters-in-law to organize their households and parenting practices with little influence from their mothers-in-law is made possible because of the support and agreement of their husbands.

Working with Chinese American Women and Their Mothers-in-Law

Practitioners and therapists need to be aware of the situation-dependent nature of family power dynamics. Power should be understood as an ongoing process and not a zero-sum game. Power dynamics and outcomes shift across time and in different situations, and who has the most power in any given relationship can also change. Therapists working with Chinese American women and their mothers-in-law also need to consider hidden power dynamics rather than focus solely on power outcomes of who wins an argument. Conflicts (e.g., an argument) may not be observable because a daughter-in-law may have anticipated the needs of her mother-in-law and behaved accordingly so as to avoid potential conflicts. Or a daughter-in-law may have accepted an undesirable situation without voicing her concerns to her mother-in-law out of a sense of futility or fear of negative repercussions. Therefore, it is important for therapists to assess whether a daughter-in-law feels she can raise issues or implement desired changes in her relationship with her mother-in-law without negative consequences.

When working with Chinese American women and their mothers-in-law, therapists should also consider how emotional economies inform power dynamics in their relationships. Feelings of entitlement, obligation, gratitude, and resentment need to be made explicit in the process. A daughter-in-law who receives assistance from her mother-in-law may be unwilling or unable to voice her displeasure or desire for change because she depends on and is grateful for such service. She may feel indebted to her mother-in-law and reluctant to overtly challenge her advice, thus reducing her power vis-à-vis the older woman. When a daughter-in-law (or mother-in-law) describes feeling obligated to provide or coerced into providing services or attention to the other, or resents doing so, it could be an indicator of less power.

Therapists should be cognizant of the power the husbands/sons hold in these families. This study points to the important role of the husband/son; he acts as the mediator rather than the instigator of conflicts between his mother and wife. Chinese American women in this study seemed to rely on their husbands' support in negotiating with their mothers-in-law, especially in the realm of childrearing and childcare. Some women express despair and resentment when they feel their husbands are not willing to support them or mediate strained relationships with the mothers-in-law. Spousal support thus acts as an important resource for women who feel powerless vis-à-vis their mothers-in-law. Therapists should engage men to mediate the relationships when working with Chinese American women and their mothers-in-law. The role a husband plays in family discord is important not only with regard to how the disagreement is resolved, but also how his handling of the situation may shape future family interactions.

As shown in the interview accounts of some Chinese American daughters-in-law, the strategy of front-stage compliance and backstage resistance seems to be a common strategy in Chinese culture, as well as any family system that emphasizes the formal display of respect toward elders. Practitioners and therapists who work with Chinese American (as well as other Asian American) daughters-in-law and mothers-in-law need to be aware of both backstage as well as front-stage behaviors to be able to capture and address covert forms of resistance that occur behind the scenes. When a daughter-in-law complies with the wishes of her mother-in-law in her presence, it does not necessarily mean she is powerless vis-à-vis her mother-in-law. It may be a strategy she uses to avoid open conflict and to achieve her goals for gaining some control over her household. It is essential for therapists and clinicians to not assume that ritualistic displays of deference in public or among extended family translate into powerlessness in the private realms. It is important for therapists to explore what a daughter-in-law does on the backstage when her mother-in-law is not present. This is particularly so when working with individuals who come from a culture that places much emphasis on formal displays of respect and familial honor in public.

References

Blood, R., & Wolfe, D. (1960). *Husbands and wives: The dynamics of married living*. New York, NY: Free Press.
Bryan, C. M., Conger, R. D., & Meehan, J. M. (2001). The influence of in-laws on change in marital success. *Journal of Marriage and the Family, 63,* 614–627.
Cotterill, P. (1994). *Friendly relations? Mothers and their daughters-in-law*. London: Taylor & Francis.
Glaser, B. G. (1965). The constant comparative method of qualitative analysis. *Social Problems, 12,* 436–445.
Globerman, J. (1996). Motivations to care: Daughters- and sons-in-law caring for relatives with Alzheimer's disease. *Family Relations, 45,* 37–45.
Goetting, A. (1990). Patterns of support among in-laws in the United States: A review of research. *Journal of Family Issues, 11*(1), 67–90.
Hochschild, A. (1989). *The second shift*. New York: Penguin.
Jackson, J., & Berg-Cross, L. (1988). Extending the extended family: The mother-in-law and daughter-in-law relationship of Black women. *Family Relations, 37,* 293–297.
Komter, A. (1989). Hidden power in marriage. *Gender & Society, 3,* 187–216.
Lee, E., Spitze, G., & Logan, J. R. (2003). Social support to parents-in-law: The interplay of gender and kin hierarchies. *Journal of Marriage and Family, 65,* 396–403.
Lopata, H. (1999). In-laws and the concept of family. *Marriage & Family Review, 28,* 161–172.
Lukes, S. (1974). *Power: A radical view*. London: Macmillan.
Pyke, K. (1999). The micropolitics of care in relationships between aging parents and adult children: Individualism, collectivism, and power. *Journal of Marriage and Family, 61,* 661–673.
Shih, K., & Pyke, K. (2010). Power, resistance, and emotional economies in women's relationships with mothers-in-law in Chinese immigrant families. *Journal of Family Issues, 31*(3), 333–357.
Shih, K. Y., & Pyke, K. (2015). Seeing mothers-in-law through the lens of the mothering ideology: An interview analysis of Taiwanese, Taiwanese American, and Mexican American daughters-in-law. *Journal of Family Issues.*
Shuey, K., & Hardy, M. A. (2003). Assistance to aging parents and parents-in-law: Does lineage affect family allocation decisions? *Journal of Marriage and Family, 65,* 418–431.
Turner, M. J., Young, C. R., & Black, K. I. (2006). Daughters-in-law and mothers-in-law seeking their place within the family: A qualitative study of differing viewpoints. *Family Relations, 55,* 588–600.
Walker, A. J. (2000). Refracted knowledge: Viewing families through the prism of social science. *Journal of Marriage and the Family, 62,* 595–608.
Wilson, A. E., Shuey, K. M., & Elder, G. H., Jr. (2003). Ambivalence in the relationship of adult children to aging parents and in-laws. *Journal of Marriage and Family, 65,* 1055–1072.

Chapter 3
Through Religion: Working-Class Korean Immigrant Women Negotiate Patriarchy

Seongeun Kim

Religion serves as an important instrument in the lives of women, particularly as a tool to help them to deal with problems arising from patriarchal marriages and to negotiate gender relations (Brusco 1995; Chen 2005; Chong 2006; Griffith 1997; Mariz and Machado 1997). Studies on Asian American women and religion show that middle-class Asian American women refashion their marital and family relationships through religion, especially to increase their autonomy and power (Kurien 1999; Chen 2005). Kurien (1999) shows that although Hindu congregations were patriarchal, professional Hindu American women gained more power and autonomy, and were more likely to establish egalitarian marital relationships, than were Hindu women in India. These women, who are critical transmitters of the Hindu and Indian cultures in their communities, construct a culture stressing men's responsibilities for family.

By stressing women's interpretations of conservative religion in unusually liberating and empowering ways, this body of research addresses immigrant women's creative ways of using religion in their marriages (Chen 2005; Kurien 1999). However, a question raised in the research is whether working-class Asian American women use religion the same way as middle-class Asian American women do. Thus the purpose of this chapter is to explore how working-class Korean immigrant Christian women living in the United States employ religion to navigate their marriages, which are very steeped in patriarchal traditions.

This is a revised version of Kim, S. (2010). Korean American women navigating marriage through evangelical Christianity. *Journal of Comparative Family Studies, 41(5)*, 735–748. This chapter is reprinted with permission of the Journal of Comparative Family Studies, all rights reserved. Do not copy or print in any format. Copyright Journal of Comparative Family Studies."

S. Kim (✉)
Sungkyunkwan University, Seoul, South Korea
e-mail: healthyfamilykim@gmail.com

K.M.-T. Quek and S.-R.S. Fang (eds.), *Transition and Change in Collectivist Family Life*, AFTA SpringerBriefs in Family Therapy,
DOI 10.1007/978-3-319-50679-1_3

Gender Relations in Working-Class Asian American Families

Studies on working-class Asian American families (Espiritu 1997, 2003; Glenn 1985; Kibria 1993) show that employed working-class Asian American women prioritize the collectivistic goal of the family unit's economic survival over gaining independence or autonomy from their husbands or partners. In the United States, men of color may have extremely limited economic opportunities and consequently, their incomes are sometimes insufficient to provide for their families. In these situations, their Asian American wives commonly work outside of the home, making it a priority to pool their income with their husbands' earnings for the family's survival (Espiritu 1997, 2003; Glenn 1985; Kibria 1993; Moon 2003). In such a context, these women tend not to be able to increase the marital power gained from earning incomes in order to change the division of household labor (Espiritu 1997, 2003; Kibria 1993; Moon 2003).

Nevertheless, as working-class Asian American women earn more money outside the home, conflict, and tension in their marriages often ensues. As a result, husbands tend to resist their wives' growing economic power (Espiritu 1997, 2003; Min 1998): many working-class Korean American men expect their wives to do household work and continue to serve them (Min 1998). In response to the strain on their marriages and their husbands' resistance to change the power dynamics at home, some Korean American women try to avoid confrontation with their husbands so as to maintain harmonious family relationships (Lim 1997; Min 1998).

While working-class Asian American women's paid work and resultant income may be important to the family, they are not absolved of housework due to their breadwinning activity as men would be. Typically these women retain responsibility for the household and add the role of workforce employee to their domestic duties. They continue to place their families' survival above their own struggle with their husbands (Espiritu 2003). In short, martial power is not fairly distributed for these women. In contrast, middle-class Asian American couples in which both partners are working experience more egalitarian gender relations than low-income couples, which is mainly due to the smaller income differential between the partners and middle-class women's success in challenging their husbands' involvement in housework (Espiritu 2003).

While working-class Korean American men have more power in their marriages due to the influence of patriarchal ideology, middle-class Asian American women have been successful in practicing egalitarian values in their martial relationships. How do working-class Korean immigrant women continue to be in a position of lesser power despite being employed? This chapter attempts to address this dilemma using religion as a resource, because religion, specifically Christianity, remains influential in the South Korean community in the United States.

My interest in this topic stems from my research trajectory of working with Korean American families and gender. I am a South Korean who has taught courses in the Human Development and Family Studies program at a public university in

United States and currently teaches in South Korea. While in the United States, I was intrigued by the ways that Korean immigrant women living in the United States use their Christian faith to bargain with patriarchy.

Method

I conducted this research with a sample of seventeen working-class Korean American Christian women in the Mid-Atlantic region of the United States. The descriptor "Korean American Christian women" indicates first-generation Korean immigrant women who came to the United States as adults and who believe in the quintessence of being Christians, to confess their sins and to have faith in Christ as their Savior. Also, all of these women were in marital relationships at the time of the research, and none of the women had any history of divorce or remarriage. Additionally, "working-class women" refers to women who are "employed in a position with little or no managerial authority and that does not require highly complex, educationally certified (i.e., college-level) skills" (Lareau 2003, p. 278).

I used in-depth interviews to gather data on the research questions, and I asked about the following four topics: (1) the women's immigration and work experiences, (2) their Christian identity and faith, (3) their husbands' involvement in housework, parenting and religious activities, and (4) the women's relationships with their husbands and the influences of religion on those marital relationships. I used grounded theory methodology to collect and analyze data (Corbin and Strauss 2008).

Results

Navigating Patriarchal Marriage Through Christianity

The findings from this research show that working-class Korean American Christian women use religion to handle the problems of patriarchal marriage and to improve their family life. For these women, religion is a vital tool not only to deal with their husbands' traditional gender practices but also to implicitly influence their husbands to be more responsible and more religious family men.

Particularly, these women utilize specific Christian teachings preached in Korean churches to interpret their own and their husbands' gendered practices, and to further develop strategies to tolerate marital problems. As they gain new Christian teachings, these women's strategies include: (1) changing their own gender role expectations with regard to their husbands' religious values and commitment, (2) taking primary responsibility for housework, (3) becoming submissive, and (4) creating invisible resistance to their husbands. Through it all, working-class

Korean immigrant women maintain the status quo of gender relations within their marriages and suppress the desire to explicitly challenge their husbands. However, these women experience a perspective shift, viewing their gendered practices as ways to transform their husbands to be more involved with family and religion.

Changing Their Own Gender Role Expectations with Regard to Husbands' Religious Values and Commitment

Ten women (59%) rarely challenged their husbands to increase their involvement in parenting and with family, thus maintaining their current gendered marital structure. Although these women were dissatisfied with their husbands' participation in housework and limited time for parenting, they tended not to express their displeasure, trying to make their marriage calm and conflict free. Instead, they creatively found ways to frame their husbands' involvement as parents. They considered how their husbands adopted Christian values in parenting practices. Some of these Christian traditions and values included praying for children, treating children as gifts from God, being a less controlling father, and supporting the development of the children's Christian identity. As long as their husbands adopted Christian parenting principles, these women learned to tolerate their husbands' lack of involvement in other areas of family life. For example, although Jin-Yong wished her husband (an employee at a dry cleaner) could be a better provider economically, she did not let his low income bother her. Very importantly, she took into account how he treated their children with respect and love. These are core values in parenting. Additionally, he provided some instrumental care for their children when needed. Her frustration increased when she sought more involvement in shared parenting. However, she found peace when she was able to reframe her expectations of her husband to being a man of biblical faith and a good Christian father to their children. She said

> He really respects his kids and treats them very nicely. Unlike many other Korean fathers [who are very authoritarian and controlling], he neither nags nor controls over his kids. He does not nag at all! Well, when I compare my husband with other men who are very capable, earn a lot of money, and speak English fluently, he is not that great. But, I really believe that he provides more important things to his kids [raising kids with evangelical teachings]. Sometimes, I wish my husband was able to give more things to his kids; if he can speak English fluently and better, it would be really nice. But, he really loves his kids and I value it more than his economic capability as a father and husband.

Not only did these women reframe gender role expectations for their husbands' practice of Christian values in parenting, but they also saw their husbands' involvement in local Korean churches as an important component in their marital relationships. They believed their husbands' participation in Korean churches, either as lay leaders or members of any service committee, provided a good foundation for them to become and remain Christian family men. It was through their husbands' involvement in religion that their children learned about altruism, and it was because of their leadership roles in the church that husbands refrained from anti-family behaviors such as smoking, drinking, or spending more time out with friends than with the family. Women whose husbands already made commitments to church service rarely placed additional demands on their husbands in terms of family responsibility and involvement, and even expressed feeling that their husbands could not devote as much time to the family because they had to be involved in their churches.

Although studies on religions and Korean immigrants show that male-centered hierarchical church structures are oppressive to Korean women (Kim 1996, 1997; Kim and Kim 2001; Kim et al. 2001; Lee 2001; Moon 2003; Park 2001), many women in this study supported their husbands' involvement in church leadership. For these women, their husbands' church leadership roles symbolize strong Christian manhood and faithfulness to God and the Korean immigrant community. However, these women indicated that at times they were ambivalent about their husbands' decision to sometimes prioritize church over taking care of the family. Nevertheless, the women let go of their wishes.

Taking Primary Responsibility for Housework

All the women in this study wanted their husbands to bear more responsibility with regard to housework, but they themselves took primary responsibility for the vast majority of household chores and family care. These women did the day-to-day domestic tasks, including meal preparation, disciplining children, planning and managing housework, and emotionally and physically caring for their families and children, with occasional help from their husbands with vacuuming, garbage disposal, or washing dishes.

However, women experienced struggles and tension as a result of being responsible for the bulk of the domestic labor in their families. Five women (29%) mentioned that, although they were working outside of the home, their husbands strongly resisted helping out with housework, and consequently they had to accommodate and adjust to their husbands' resistance. To deal with their husbands' lack of cooperation, these women used Christian teachings that emphasized harmonious marriages. Mi-Sun struggled for about 10 years to get her husband to help with household chores, often encountering severe tension between her husband and herself. Sadly, all her efforts were in vain. She eventually accepted that her husband refused to help out at home and she tried to accept the status quo as to gender relations by adhering to religious teachings in order to avoid conflict in their marital relationship. She states

> I always thought that I was miserable because my husband did not help at home after he came from work. I worked so hard for our family's livelihood here in the U.S. and in Korea. I always complained about his lack of involvement in housework and parenting my kids. I fought against him all the time. But I learned that it did not work at all, and my husband did not change even a bit. One day, when I was in the church, I heard a sermon, and it hit

> my mind. My pastor said that God sent perfect husbands for us, and since then, I realized that he might be the perfect person for me. Well, I don't know if it is a healthy way of keeping marriage, but I think I have to accept him as he is. I struggled about this issue more than ten years. We fought unbelievably many times, especially when I could not stand my husband. But I think God changed my mind to accept him for who he is, and I am at peace since then. I even regretted that I challenged my husband for about ten years, and if I had just accepted, I would not have wasted this ten-year-period of struggles.

Although the rest of the women also viewed themselves as the primary doers of housework, they mentioned that their husbands made some adjustments after the women appealed to their husbands on the basis that they (the women) had worked outside the home since their move to the United States. Their husbands' participation in housework was minimal, such as washing the dishes, vacuuming, folding laundry, or getting some shopping done for these women, but they felt that their husbands' contributions were enough. In doing so, they avoided conflict in their marriages.

Becoming Submissive

Korean American Christian women in this study mentioned that as their faith and reliance on Christian teachings grew, they had become less confrontational and resistant to their husbands in dealing with marital conflict. These women, who used to raise their voices and resist their husbands when marital conflicts arose, came to realize that their overt challenges only hurt their husbands' egos without resolving the problem. Rather than resorting to confrontation, they gradually turned to Christian teachings for guidance about attaining peaceful resolutions and keeping harmonious family relationships.

These women discussed their decisions to change the manner in which they dealt with marital conflict and became submissive to their husbands in relation to their identity as mothers and as Christian spouses. About six women (35%) mentioned that it was mainly for the sake of their children that they refrained from challenging their husbands and creating conflict in their marriages. Some had even contemplated or attempted to divorce their husbands because of their husbands' hierarchical and highly traditional attitudes toward women. However, they made maximum efforts to preserve their marriages because they needed the "husbands' hands" and financial contribution for their children's well-being. In such circumstances, these women utilized Christian teachings that addressed not sinning while angry and wifely submission to deal with marital conflict. Some wives viewed their submission as a way to improve their families and felt compelled to endure difficult martial relations instead of pushing for a greater domestic labor contribution from the husbands. Most of them (N = 11, 65%) attributed their avoidance of conflict and their submission to their husbands as a way to maintain their Christian identity. Some even believed that challenging their husbands was against God's will.

Ironically, these women found that in becoming more submissive, they moved away from contentious behaviors, which resulted in not threatening their husbands' egos, and thus their husbands listened and respected them more. The husbands' positive behavior changes confirmed and reinforced these women's subservience to their husbands, which in turn impacted the wives' responses to conflict: "they lowered their voices in times of conflict" Jin-Yong said that she was extremely lucky to have her husband because he was a caring husband and father. When he awakened his two daughters, he hugged and kissed them, and most importantly, he prayed for them to have bright days. However, on occasions when she felt the need to complain about his insensitivity toward her, she stopped from doing so as she recalled Christian teachings regarding contentiousness.

Creating Invisible Resistance to the Husbands

Although these women, influenced by Christian teachings, tended to be accommodating to their husbands, they covertly challenged and have been challenging their husbands to become Christian family men. They believed that religious and spiritual transformation and maturity provided their husbands with strong Christian moral standards to guide them in their roles as fathers and husbands.

Without damaging their husbands' egos, these women tried to subtly and invisibly challenge their husbands, mostly through prayers. Focusing their eyes on the God of hope, they saw prayer as the surest way to influence their husbands. In particular, those women whose husbands were neglecting their responsibility to earn a living and were abandoning the family have relied greatly on prayer to reform their husbands. Although Gum-Sook's husband has not been a bad provider, since both of them run a dry cleaning operation, he was frequently out drinking and playing poker games, sometimes staying out until early in the morning. Before her husband became a Christian several years ago, she had prayed and cried out to God to deal with her husband's alcoholism and negligence toward their family. She strongly believed that her prayers for her husband's salvation, spoken over the course of more than ten years, really transformed him. Although she is not completely satisfied with the person he is, at least she had less trouble in her marriage because her husband was no longer an alcoholic and ceased his emotional abuse. She mentioned

> Well, I could not change him, but my Christian faith did. He is so much better now. He was an atheist, but as he became a Christian, he has gotten better… But, he is still bad… I had to endure my husband's negligence for his family. There were so many times when I felt that I could not live with him any longer, really. Also, he is extremely temperamental unlike me, and I could not handle him at all. And, he did not do anything to take care of his kids. He was extremely bad… I heavily relied on my faith and prayer. I did not have anybody I could rely on here in the U.S. except my two aunts. My parents and brothers were all in Korea. I am not the kind of person who easily talks about my stuff to people, and I only talked to one of my aunts. But, when I got deeply frustrated and was in despair, I prayed hard to God and cried out loud to Him. I could not talk to my mother because I did not want

> my mother to worry about me. Also, I did not want my younger brothers to worry about me. To whom could I ask for help? God was the only one. I prayed so hard… [crying] I really believe that the changes that happened in my family were all God's work, and I am greatly thankful to Him.

Prayers are an important tool that women use to reform husbands and inspire their husbands' leadership (Griffith 1997), though this does not necessarily mean that Korean Christian women in this study believed their husbands to be the spiritual leaders of the home. Even though their husbands may not have borne greater responsibility for leadership within the household, however, these women nevertheless believed prayers have helped their husbands to be more involved with their families. For instance, ever since Kyung-su married, her husband has been neglecting his responsibility as the head of the family, spending money recklessly on gambling, severely abusing her emotionally, committing adultery, and being in and out of employment. She contemplated leaving him. However, her firm belief in and hope for her husband's spiritual transformation led her to endure all these difficulties in her marriage. To the best of her ability, she persisted in her efforts to bring her husband before God so that he might experience spiritual transformation. These working-class Korean American women believed that prayer would bring about spiritual transformation, ultimately making their husbands more responsible.

Relatedly and consistently, in their daily interactions, some of the women refrained from any behavior that would contribute to their husbands' loss of interest in and commitment to the Christian faith. For example, these women have reduced their involvement at church if their husbands expressed displeasure about the wives being too committed to their church-related events.

Discussion

Based on the above stories, I can see that working-class Korean American women residing in the United States are very conflicted because of how traditional patriarchal conceptions of marriage and heterosexual gender roles conflict with the difficult reality of handling work both outside and within the home. The old, deep-seated belief system dies hard, and it has been an uphill battle for these women on a daily basis. They are not able to trade their income for a corresponding reduction in their household chores and parenting tasks. The stress they encounter takes its toll on them and their relationships. Looking for resources from within, they resort to using religion to handle their problems. These women are devout Christians who seek Christian teachings and principles on gender and human relationships to cope with life's challenges. Religion is a powerful resource that shapes their perceptions of their husbands, and it is a channel used to move their husbands to become more engaged in their marriages and family life.

Competencies for Counseling Working-Class Korean Immigrant Christian Women

Therapists should be aware that, unlike middle-class Asian American women who use religion to reject some of the traditional demands imposed on them and to gain power and autonomy in their marriages (Chen 2005; Kurien 1999), working-class Korean American Christian women may use religion in more accommodative ways. In terms of dealing with their husbands' traditional gender beliefs and practices, these women accept traditional gender relations reinforced by the religious teachings of their faith. At the same time, they use religion to change their husbands into more responsible and more involved family men, but they do so covertly. Religion serves an important function in supporting these women implicitly in their attempts to persuade their husbands to become committed to their marriages and involved in family life.

First, therapists who are working with Christian Asian American women need to be aware that their use of religion in marriage may be class specific, and therefore therapists will need to explore how some Asian American women of different social classes view their religious beliefs. It should not be assumed that the meaning of religion in the lives of these women is the same across different social classes. It is critical for therapists to attend to the significance of religion for the women they serve and the complex ways they interpret religious teachings and apply faith in their marriages.

Second, therapists need to focus on the gender context of working-class Korean immigrant women and their marriages. These women make significant financial contributions to the family, but their husbands resist increasing their own participation in housework and childrearing. In such marriage conditions, women experience great tension and internal struggle, as they feel forced to accept the status quo as to gender relations and suppress their desire to explicitly challenge their husbands. Dealing with the tension and internal struggle involved in navigating patriarchal marriage is painful and burdensome. Therapists should attend to these women's struggles and challenges, and seek ways to empower them using resources from within their cultural background.

Third, when working with Korean husbands and wives, therapists should consider their socialization in the patriarchal structure and find ways to attend to the immigrant women's culture-specific ways of negotiating gender. These women's submission and covert ways of challenging their husbands using religion is deeply rooted in Confucian ideology about family and gender relations, which stresses women's "total obedience and endurance as a prerequisite for family harmony and cohesion" (Chong 2006, p. 714). Therapists can encourage both women and their husbands to come to the therapy sessions together and in particular, help husbands understand why and how their wives resort to religion as a coping mechanism. Further, therapists could encourage husbands to resist cultural beliefs and messages that place the responsibility for familial harmony on women.

Finally, therapists can promote gender equality in dual-career couples as they seek to understand the meanings and use of religion in the lives of Asian American Christian women of different social classes. It is especially important for therapists to intentionally position themselves to enable these women's struggles and pain to be heard by their husbands (Knudson-Martin 2012). Getting the husbands to understand how the women use religion to make accommodations and to sacrifice for the survival of their families would promote equality in the couple's relationship.

References

Brusco, E. (1995). *The reformation of machismo: Evangelical conversion and gender in Columbia*. Austin, TX: University of Texas Press.

Chen, C. (2005). A self of one's own: Taiwanese immigrant women and religious conversions. *Gender & Society, 19*(3), 336–357.

Chong, K. (2006). Negotiating patriarch: South Korean evangelical women and the politics of gender. *Gender & Society, 20*(6), 697–724.

Corbin, J., & Strauss, A. (2008). *Basics of qualitative research: techniques and procedures for developing grounded theory* (3rd ed.). Thousands Oak, CA: Sage.

Espiritu, Y. (1997). *Asian American women and men: Labors, laws, and love*. Thousands Oak, CA: Sage.

Espiritu, Y. (2003). Gender and labor in Asian immigrant families. In P. Hondagneu-Sotelo (Ed.), *Gender and U.S. immigration: Contemporary trends* (pp. 81–100). Berkeley, CA: University of California Press.

Glenn, E. (1985). Racial ethnic women's labor: The intersection of race, gender and class oppression. *Review of Racial Political Economics, 17*(3), 86–108.

Griffith, M. (1997). *God's daughters: Evangelical women and the power of submission*. London, England: University of California Press.

Kibria, N. (1993). *Family tightrope: The changing lives of Vietnamese Americans*. Princeton, NJ: Princeton University Press.

Kim, A. (1996). *Women struggling for a new life: The role of religion in the cultural passage from Korea to America*. Albany, NY: State University of New York Press.

Kim, J. (1997). *Bridge-makers and cross-bearers: Korean-American women and the church*. Atlanta, GA: Scholars Press.

Kim, K. C., & Kim, S. (2001). Ethnic roles of Korean immigrant churches in the United States. In H. Kwon, K.C. Kim & R.S. Warner (Eds.), *Korean Americans and religions: Pilgrims and missionaries from a different shore* (pp. 71–94). University Park, PA: Pennsylvania State University Press.

Kim, K. C., Warner, R. S., & Kwon, H. (2001). Korean American religion in international perspective. In H. Kwon., K.C. Kim & R.S. Warner (Eds.), *Korean American and religions: Pilgrims and missionaries from a different shore* (pp. 3–24). University Park, PA: Pennsylvania State University Press.

Knudson-Martin, C. (2012). Changing gender norms in families and society. In F. Walsh. (Ed.), *Normal family processes: Growing diversity and complexity* (pp 324–326). New York, NY: Guilford.

Kurien, P. (1999). Gendered ethnicity: creating a Hindu Indian identity in the United States. *American Behavioral Scientist 42*, 648–670.

Lareau, A. (2003). *Unequal childhoods: Class, race, and family life*. Berkeley, CA: California.

Lee, S. H. (2001). Pilgrimage and home in the wilderness of marginality: symbols and context in Asian American theology. In H. Kwon., K.C. Kim & R.S. Warner (Eds.), *Korean Americans and religions: Pilgrims and missionaries from a different shore* (pp. 55–70). University Park, PA: Pennsylvania State University Press.

Lim, I. (1997). Korean immigrant women's challenge to gender inequality at home: The interplay of economic resources, gender, and family. *Gender & Society, 11* (1), 31–51.

Mariz, C. L., & Machado, M. D. (1997). Pentecostalism and women in Brazil. In E. L. Cleary & H. W. West-Gambino (Eds.), *Power, politics, and Pentecostalism in Latin America.* Westview: Boulder, CO.

Min, P. (1998). *Changes and conflict: Korean immigrant families in New York.* Needham Heights, MA: Allyn and Bacon.

Moon, S. (2003). Immigration and mothering: Case studies from two generations of Korean immigrant women. *Gender and Society, 17*(6), 840–860.

Park, S. (2001). The intersection of religion, race, gender, and ethnicity in the identity formation of Korean American evangelical women. In H. Kwon, K.C. Kim & R.S. Warner (Eds.), *Korean Americans and religions: pilgrims and missionaries from a different shore* (pp. 193-208). University Park, PA: Pennsylvania State University Press.

Chapter 4
Bridging the Relational Space Between First- and Second-Generation Chinese American Christians

Jessica ChenFeng

In the literature about the family and relational health needs of Asians and Asian Americans, there is a gap when it comes to researching Chinese American Christians (Atwood and Conway 2004; Benner and Kim 2009; Hung Hisu and Ng 2002; Kim et al. 2014; Lam and Chan-So 2014; Lim et al. 2009). 31% of Chinese Americans identify as being Christian (Pew Forum on Religion and Public Life 2012); this is the largest religious group for Chinese Americans, even higher than those who identify with Buddhism or other religions (Yang 1999).

My interest in this topic is very much connected to my experiences growing up in Southern California as a second-generation Chinese/Taiwanese American Christian. Based on my experience as well as the literature, I know that first- and second-generation Chinese American Christian families face many of the same challenges that other Asian immigrants face: intergenerational conflict, acculturation difficulties, the stress of being a minority in a majority European-American cultural context (Lee et al. 2009; Min and Yang Sao 2005; Park 2008). At the same time, our families have found unique support in the Chinese Christian community. However, it is unclear exactly how the Christian faith intersects with intergenerational dynamics in Chinese American families. Thus the purpose of this study is to understand this intersection so that family therapists can better connect with the cultural, generational, and spiritual ways of pursuing health and wellness for this population.

This chapter is a revised version of ChenFeng, J, Knudson-Martin, C., & Nelson, T. (2015). Intergenerational tension, connectedness and separateness in the lived experience of first and second generation Chinese American Christians. *Contemporary Family Therapy*. DOI:10.1007/s10591-015-9335-9.

J. ChenFeng (✉)
Department of Educational Psychology and Counseling, California State University, Northridge, CA, USA
e-mail: jessica.chen@csun.edu

K.M.-T. Quek and S.-R.S. Fang (eds.), *Transition and Change in Collectivist Family Life*, AFTA SpringerBriefs in Family Therapy,
DOI 10.1007/978-3-319-50679-1_4

Intergenerational Dynamics and the Chinese Church

In this study, the term "first generation" refers to Chinese parents who immigrated from Taiwan, Shanghai, Canton, Hong Kong, Beijing, and Korea; "second generation" is used to describe adult children who were born and raised in the American context; and "1.5 generation" refers to now-adult children who arrived in the United States as children or adolescents. Existing research on intergenerational relationships has tended to focus on the intergenerational strains related to acculturation differences (Lee et al. 2005; Tsai-Chae and Nagata 2008), parenting styles and warmth (Juang et al. 2007; Lim et al. 2009), and differences in cultural expectations (Chung 2001; Tsai-Chae and Nagata 2008). The differences between the first and second generations are often framed as an issue of collectivism versus individualism, Eastern versus Western ideologies, and controlling versus flexible parenting (Cheah et al. 2013; Lee et al. 2014; Lim et al. 2009). Quantitative studies on intergenerational conflict highlight negative impacts on the second generation, including lower self-esteem, depression, indecisiveness about career, and behavioral problems (e.g., Juang et al. 2007; Lee et al. 2005). The majority of these quantitative studies, however, focus on the experiences of youth and college students. Very little is known about the relationships that second-generation adults have with their first-generation parents using a qualitative method. Even less research has been done to understand relationships between immigrant Chinese and U.S.-born Chinese who are socialized in a Christian environment.

Little is known about what happens when Chinese American families become or grow up as part of the Chinese American church. Chinese churches support families by providing alternative ways of living out family life. For instance, pastors might challenge traditional Chinese parenting styles by encouraging more open communication between parents and children and less controlling parenting techniques (Chen 2006). The church also shapes how Chinese American families face problems; the church may reframe the meaning of cultural values. For example, reframing the concept of saving face can reduce the stigma associated with seeking mental health support (Cao 2005). These are just some of the ways the Christian church may significantly impact Chinese American families.

Method

I approached this study as someone who comes from within the community of Chinese American Christians, as I grew up in a close-knit Chinese/Taiwanese American church. For this study, I engaged two colleagues, Carmen Knudson-Martin and Timothy Nelson, both of European-American heritage, who are interested in the larger social context and justice. I contacted pastors and leaders of Chinese and Asian American churches, and through snowball sampling, 16 participants across churches of various Christian denominations volunteered to be interviewed. Participants self-identified as Christians and English speakers. I interviewed eight first-generation participants and eight second-generation participants, with an equal number of male and female participants in each generation. The ages of first-generation parents ranged from 49 to 59 years old, and the ages of second-generation adult children ranged from 29 to 34 years old. Participants identified as being Chinese and Taiwanese in ethnicity, with family history in Taiwan, Shanghai, Canton, Hong Kong, Beijing, and Korea. I applied interpretative phenomenology for the analysis process (Smith et al. 2009).

Intergenerational Tension and Disconnection

A recurring theme that surfaced was that both generations each felt that the other generation did not or could not understand their own generation's experiences because they were raised in different contexts. The phenomenon of immigration created a generational culture gap, resulting in first-generation parents being shaped by one sociocultural context and the second generation being shaped by a different (American) sociocultural context. The consequences of this generational difference are tension and disconnection. There is tension because there seems to be a longing to connect, and at the same time, an awareness of loss—no matter how much effort is made, one generation may never feel truly known or understood by the other generation. This in turn causes a feeling of disconnection. Many first-generation parents expressed that their children would never understand a significant piece of who the parents are. For example, Kelly is a Taiwan-born, 55-year-old mother who raised her son through a difficult divorce. She spoke of her sadness about the disconnect she feels with her adult son:

> I reach out to my [son], but he doesn't want me to reach out to him, and I just feel that the more I pursue, the more I push him away. And my generation is hardest because we still have that traditional foundation in us, which we want to instill into the next generation. But the next generation, they grew up here. It's American here. They will not understand where we came from. So it's kind of sad. It feels like you lost that culture because they will never understand.

In a similar way, the second-generation adult children spoke of not being understood by their parents. They discussed how their choices (e.g., regarding spouses, career, college, church) would often collide with their parents' expectations. Helen is a Taiwan-born 28-year-old who immigrated to the United States at age eleven. She expressed the hurt and disconnect she experienced in her relationship with her parents because it was difficult for them to accept the things that are important to her:

> They weren't very supportive of my fiancé because he's not Taiwanese and he doesn't speak Chinese… They would always make snide comments like "If we just kept you in Taiwan or did this or that, you'd be getting married to a Taiwanese person." And they constantly compare my pending nuptials with other people whom they know in Taiwan

> who married other Taiwanese people… I think it's just very uncomfortable for them to open up their home to someone of a different culture even if he is Asian.

This lack of knowledge and understanding exhibited by each generation toward the other generation's contextual experiences has been associated with increased generational tension and greater disconnection. Participants responded to their experiences of tension and disconnection in one of two ways—either they created a special intergenerational connection or they encountered separateness with that generation.

Intergenerational Connectedness

The term "connectedness" reflects the experience participants had of pursuing a more active, engaging relationship with their other-generation family member(s). It is worth noting that all of the second-generation participants shared about maintaining a sense of connectedness with their parents. Intergenerational connectedness can be subcategorized into two ways of responding to the tension/disconnect: (1) mutual acceptance and (2) adaptive pursuit.

Mutual acceptance. Both generations of participants in this category seemed to accept and find peace with intergenerational disconnect. There have been cultural or spiritual differences between the generations, but this did not create relationship distress. Because of how they sought to live out their Christian faith, persons in this category were proactive in trying to grow and connect with members of the other generation.

First generation. Jennifer exemplifies a Christian mother who wants to live in a way that honors her beliefs in God. Jennifer is a 56-year-old married mother of three adult children. She primarily sees her role as the parent through the lens of her Christian faith, more so than through Taiwanese culture. When confronted with her own cultural assumptions or expectations, she is willing to consider making changes in light of her Christian faith in order to connect with her children:

> Everything that we do, God is the center… I always tell [my children], "As long as you are walking in God's way, that's all we ask." It's never like "I want this. I don't want you to marry this. I don't want you to do that," [but instead,] "What is it that God wants for you?"… One time I came home from work and I opened the door and [my younger son] said, "Mom is home!" He ran into his room and he was trying to tidy up his room. I will always remember that day… I don't want to come home and have my kids behave like that… Those are little lessons here and there that help me as a mom to learn that what I was doing is not right and I need to change.

Second generation. Five second-generation participants experience mutual acceptance with their parents. They seem to be able to let go of past frustrations and make intentional efforts to understand their parents' different perspectives. Joshua is a 28-year-old clinical psychology resident who used to fight with his father, and he shared how his faith in God taught him to prioritize relationships and transformed the way he engages with his father:

> A huge turning point… was this incident where we were eating in front of the TV and [my father] accidentally ate my mom's share of the food… And my mom got hurt and [my father]… demanded that I give up my share to mom… I was like "What?! Really? You're not even going to apologize!?" When I gave that incredulous kind of look, he hit me. I don't think I had been slapped in the face before, so he was furious. He sent me to my room… Shortly after he came up… and he apologized. He said he was sorry and he was out of line… He had never apologized before. I started crying… it was kind of a redemptive moment.

Joshua shared about this incident because through this experience he came to better understand his father, and their relationship shifted toward one of acceptance. Though this encounter may run contrary to Chinese social norms, this process was made possible due to their shared Christian faith, which allowed for both generations to exercise humility and facilitate redemption and reconciliation.

Adaptive pursuit. Three second-generation adult children and one first-generation mother fell in this subcategory. These participants desired to connect with their other-generation family members but experienced less mutuality in their relationships. They were willing to make changes in themselves in order to preserve the relationships, even if this was not reciprocated.

First generation. Michelle is a 58-year-old divorced Chinese mother with a married daughter who is a young mother. When Michelle experiences her daughter as withdrawn, tired, and not wanting to connect, she attempts to learn better ways to engage with her daughter and son-in-law in order to maintain relationships with them. Engagement with someone who does not want to connect is not easy. But for Michelle, tolerance and humility are Christian values she exercises as she continues to seek her own growth so that she can deepen her connection with her daughter:

> With faith, sometimes I get so excited. Now I learn that I really need to gauge [my daughter's and son-in-law's] spiritual life, their condition and what stage they are in, whether they are ready for it or not. I'm learning [to wait] so that I don't share something prematurely because it will only frustrate them.

Second generation. There were three second-generation participants who seemed to long for more connection and understanding from their parents, even though their efforts were mostly unilateral. These second-generation participants felt like they were making efforts to engage their parents and understand the cultural differences at play, but that their efforts were not reciprocated. Helen, who was introduced earlier, persists in trying to better understand her parents. Though she feels hurt because her parents struggle to accept her fiancé, and though it might be easier to give up on maintaining that parent–child relationship, it is important to her to live out Christian values such as honoring her parents. She tries "to see them as loving and nurturing. So I try to give them the chance… the chance to love me, but with that chance, you become very vulnerable to being hurt by their words." She sees that "it takes a lot of time" and that even though reality is not as she wishes it were, there has been much change. Because Helen hopes and believes in God's desire for peace and reconciliation, she continues to be intentional in relating to and connecting with her parents.

Intergenerational Separateness

All of the participants who responded to intergenerational tension and disconnect with “separateness” were first-generation parents. Though the term “separateness” might imply that they wanted to remain apart, this is not the case. These parents shared that as much as they would like to communicate with their adult children more frequently, they were intentionally leaving some relational space or “separateness” between them and their adult children. This seemed to be the only way they knew how to interact with their children. They seemed to function and do life on their own while trying to hold tightly onto those parent–child relationships, missing a certain relational element in the process. The experience of “separateness” can be subcategorized into two themes: (1) clinging to faith and (2) rooted in traditional roles.

Clinging to faith. Two first-generation mothers described having this experience. They both yearn to connect more deeply with their sons, and while they make efforts to call their children and be available, they still wonder if they are good enough mothers. They get the sense that their sons do not want the sort of connection these mothers long for, which challenges how they understand their identities as mothers. As they wrestle with this, they consider the beliefs of their Christian faith and how that faith provides them identity and hope.

Tina is a 59-year-old first-generation Taiwanese mother who is married with two adult sons. While raising her two boys, she struggled to overcome language barriers and acculturation gaps. She wishes that she could be more connected to her sons and expresses a sense of deep sadness, helplessness, and desperation because she feels she cannot do anything to deepen the intimacy of those relationships:

> One thing that I… regret or… sad… [sort of] incomplete in my relationship with my kids. I didn’t participate or I don’t know if I should participate or not… I feel I didn’t participate much in their life in general. Therefore, there’s not much communication. They don’t call me that often, they don’t check on me…

Though Tina continues to wrestle with her role as a mother, her faith in God has been a source of hope and strength. It helps her envision the relationships she could have with her sons in the future:

> I just hope my kids and grandkids in the future… that they will receive God’s mercy… I really hope that I can participate in their lives… communicate and share the faith.

Rooted in traditional roles. All of the four first-generation fathers had this experience. They remained grounded in a traditional Chinese fathering role in response to intergenerational tension/disconnect. They stood firm on what they believed and understood about parenting based on their Chinese cultural background. While the mothers felt a sense of loss and sadness because of the “separateness” and thus were led to a position of “clinging to faith,” the fathers talked about this “separateness” simply as the way things have been between parents and children. Fathers demonstrated less expression of emotional impact, holding to the traditional Chinese role of what it meant to be a father—to be the breadwinner of the family. These fathers tend to respond in pragmatic ways and use reasoning as a channel for engaging their children.

Steve is a 59-year-old father of two young adult children. He sounds comfortable in his traditional fatherly identity, and even though he sees "Caucasian people" parenting differently, he remains secure in his Chinese way of parenting:

> I am [a] very traditional father. When they got some needs… I play my role. I support them and share their life in school. We tell them what kind of experiences we had in the past… to tell them… how to handle their situation… If there is no [need], [my son] is not going to call us. It is not like the Caucasian people. They have very good intimate relationship[s] between parents and children. They hug all the time.

Steve goes on to explain that he accepts that he is a Chinese father who will not always understand his children's "Caucasian" world, and that there will be circumstances under which he cannot help his adult children because they have grown up in an American context and he will not respond like American parents. Similarly, Charles, a 55-year-old architect, believes that "separateness" is developmentally appropriate. He shared, "When I was their age, I made a lot of decisions by myself. So I try to encourage [my children] to make their own decisions." These first-generation fathers seem to lack expression of warmth. In different ways, they provide "instrumental" support for their children. That is, they make sacrifices for them but also anticipated that their children would go through challenges and growth experiences in the American context as ethnic minorities.

Discussion and Clinical Implications

These stories of how first- and second-generation Chinese American Christians respond to intergenerational tension and disconnect can be summarized by four observations: (a) Even in the midst of disconnection, there was a strong desire and intention to maintain family relationships. (b) An understanding of one's Christian identity informed family relationships. (c) There were generational differences in experiences of and responses to disconnection. (d) There were gender differences in the experiences of first-generation parents.

Maintenance of Family Relationships

Even though each generation described experiencing a feeling of disconnect from the other generation, these family members did not simply let that divide them. In whatever ways they understood or knew, they guarded their family ties. The generational culture gaps were not significant enough to break family relationships, and their statements suggest that their Christian faith played a role in their efforts to maintain and preserve familial bonds.

Therefore, clinicians can practice using sociocultural attunement (Pandit et al. 2015), a clinical concept to support the understanding of the socio-contextual meanings of their clients' experiences. It is important to affirm the ways that family members maintain their relationships by exploring questions such as:

- What are they already doing that leads to intergenerational connectedness?
- What peers at church or in other support systems encourage the first-/second-generation family member to persist/be adaptive in the midst of family conflict?
- Who in their community could be a resource to help each generation to understand the other?

Additionally, it may be helpful to use a strength-based approach, which would encourage clinicians to find resources and strengths pertinent to the cultural backgrounds of these families.

Christian Identity Informing Familial Relationships

A number of the participants pointed to Christian identity as influencing who they are and how they choose to engage with family members. The Christian faith provides intrapersonal and interpersonal resources to address family conflicts as well as a foundation upon which a new family identity could be built without forfeiting the traditional Chinese values they hold most dear (e.g., honor, respect, loyalty). Within the Christian framework, parents do not have to position themselves so hierarchically to connect with children. Thus, in the spirit of mutually upholding family traditions and relationships, adult children could consider taking more initiative to connect with their parents. In clinical work, therapists can help clients explore this Christian identity with questions such as:

- What does it mean to be Christian and Chinese?
- What Christian values support them in their role as a parent/child? An identity in Christ may mean that they no longer find their primary worth in another being or thing, but rather, they know that in pain and loss, they are deeply loved by God. This worldview can provide Christians humility to be in challenging relationships while also giving them a sense of their own worth and affirming the entirety of who they are, including their cultural backgrounds.
- Therapists can also better understand how Chinese American Christian parents and children see their roles by looking at biblical texts such as the story of the Prodigal Son (Luke 15:11–32). This story highlights the love of a father for his two sons. However, both sons love the father not for who he is, but only for what he can give them. The parable invites both the first and second generation to reflect about their relationships and roles as parent/child.

Generational Differences

The two generations responded to intergenerational tension in different ways. Some first-generation mothers were active in connecting with their children, and other mothers felt a lack of closeness but remained available and found support in their Christian faith. The fathers were not surprised or as emotionally impacted by the tension and disconnect in their relationships with their children. They felt they needed to allow their adult children to learn on their own. Contrary to the first generation's parenting experiences, all the second-generation participants described feeling connected to their parents. This indicates that, upholding the cultural and Christian norm of respecting parents, these second-generation Chinese American Christians are willing to work on their relationships with their parents. In clinical practice, it would be important to validate the unique experiences and responses of both generations by asking:

- What are the hopes, dreams, and challenges of your parents' immigration story?
- How much does the second generation know about these stories and how do these stories impact them?
- What has been difficult for the second generation about being raised in a bi-cultural environment?
- How does the Christian faith change or shape how members of one generation are willing to connect with the other generation?

Gender Differences in First Generation Parents

There were also clear differences between the experiences of first-generation mothers and first-generation fathers. It seemed natural for fathers to be "separated" to provide room for children to grow, whereas mothers were more emotionally impacted by the feeling of disconnect. Therapeutically, it would be imperative to tend to the gendered ideas, influences, and expectations of mothering and fathering by asking:

- What parenting roles do mom and dad play at home?
- Where did these ideas of parenting as mother/father come from?
- How have these roles been beneficial or detrimental to building up the family? The Typology of Parent–Child Relational Orientations (TP-CRO) (Kim et al. 2014) may be a helpful guide for these conversations.

Conclusion

Based on the findings of this study, there is hope for the future as generations grow older. Though there are disconnect, loss, and tension as a result of immigration and acculturating, the influence of one's Christian faith and identity can address relational issues and foster meaningful connection between generations. This study affirms the call for therapists to consider the integration of spirituality with clinical work (Carlson et al. 2010), as well as to address the significance of religion and culture (Carneiro 2012). Because there is still little integration of support between Christian communities and mental health communities, we hope that studies like these will encourage the church and mental health field to come together to offer support to these families.

References

Atwood, J. D., & Conway, B. Y. M. (2004). Therapy with Chinese American families: A social constructionist perspective. *American Journal of Family Therapy, 32*(2), 155–172. doi:10.1080/01926180490255819.

Benner, A. D., & Kim, S. Y. (2009). Intergenerational experiences of discrimination in Chinese American families: Influences of socialization and stress. *Journal of Marriage and Family, 71*(4), 862–877. doi:10.1111/j.1741-3737.2009.00640.x.

Cao, N. (2005). The church as a surrogate family for working class immigrant Chinese youth: an ethnography of segmented assimilation. *Sociology of Religion, 66*(2), 183–200. (Accession No. ATLA0001467414)

Carlson, T. S., McGeorge, C., & Anderson, A. (2010). The importance of spirituality in couple and family therapy: A comparative study of therapists' and educators' beliefs. *Contemporary Family Therapy, 33*(1), 3–16. doi:10.1007/s10591-010-9136-0.

Carneiro, R. (2012). The impact of Christianity on therapy with Latino families. *Contemporary Family Therapy, 35*(1), 137–146. doi:10.1007/s10591-012-9209-3.

Cheah, C. S. L., Leung, C. Y. Y., & Zhou, N. (2013). Understanding "Tiger Parenting" through the perceptions of Chinese immigrant mothers: can Chinese and U.S. parenting coexist? *Asian American Journal of Psychology, 4*(1), 30–40. doi:10.1037/a0031217.

Chen, C. (2006). From filial piety to religious piety: Evangelical Christianity reconstructing Taiwanese immigrant families in the United States. *International Migration Review, 40*(3), 573–602. doi:10.1111/j.1747-7379.2006.00032.x.

ChenFeng, J., Knudson-Martin, C., & Nelson, T. (2015). Intergenerational tension, connectedness and separateness in the lived experience of first and second generation Chinese American Christians. *Contemporary Family Therapy*. doi:10.1007/s10591-015-9335-9.

Chung, R. H. G. (2001). Gender, ethnicity, and acculturation in intergenerational conflict of Asian American college students. *Cultural Diversity & Ethnic Minority Psychology, 7*(4), 376–386. doi:10.1037//1099-9809.7.4.376.

Hung Hisu, C., & Ng, K. S. (2002). The perception of resiliency mechanisms in Chinese American families: Implications for family therapy. *Family Therapy: The Journal of the California Graduate School of Family Psychology, 29*(2), 89–100. (Accession No. 2002-06041-003)

Juang, L. P., Syed, M., & Takagi, M. (2007). Intergenerational discrepancies of parental control among Chinese American families: Links to family conflict and adolescent depressive symptoms. *Journal of Adolescence, 30*(6), 965–975. doi:10.1016/j.adolescence.2007.01.004.

Kim, L., Knudson-Martin, C., & Tuttle, A. (2014). Toward relationship-directed parenting: An example of North American born second-generation Korean-American mothers and their partners. *Family Process, 53,* 55–66. doi:10.1111/famp.12052.

Lam, C. M., & Chan-So, P. C. Y. (2014). Validation of the Chinese version of differentiation of self inventory (C-DSI). *Journal of Marital and Family Therapy.* Advanced online publication. doi:10.1111/jmft.12031

Lee, E. H., Zhou, Q., Ly, J., Main, A., Tao, A., & Chen, S. H. (2014). Neighborhood characteristics, parenting styles, and children's behavioral problems in Chinese American immigrant families. *Cultural Diversity and Ethnic Minority Psychology, 20*(2), 202–212. doi:10.1037/a0034390.

Lee, R. M., Su, J., & Yoshida, E. (2005). Coping with intergenerational family conflict among Asian American college students. *Journal of Counseling Psychology, 52*(3), 389–399. doi:10.1037/0022-0167.52.3.389.

Lee, S., Juon, H.-S., Martinez, G., Hsu, C. E., Robinson, E. S., Bawa, J., et al. (2009). Model minority at risk: Expressed needs of mental health by Asian American young adults. *Journal of Community Health: The Publication for Health Promotion and Disease Prevention, 34*(2), 144–152. doi:10.1007/s10900-008-9137-1.

Lim, S.-L., Yeh, M., Liang, J., Lau, A. S., & McCabe, K. (2009). Acculturation gap, intergenerational conflict, parenting style, and youth distress in immigrant Chinese American families. *Marriage & Family Review, 45*(1), 84–106. doi:10.1080/01494920802537530.

Min, Z., & Yang Sao, X. (2005). The multifaceted American experiences of the children of Asian immigrants: Lessons for segmented assimilation. *Ethnic & Racial Studies, 28*(6), 1119–1152. doi:10.1080/01419870500224455.

Park, L. S.-H. (2008). Continuing significance of the model minority myth: The second generation. *Social Justice, 35*(2), 134–144. (Accession No. 508035759)

Smith, J. A., Flowers, P., & Larkin, M. (2009). *Interpretative phenomenological analysis: Theory, method and research.* London: SAGE Publications.

Tsai-Chae, A. H., & Nagata, D. K. (2008). Asian values and perceptions of intergenerational family conflict among Asian American students. *Cultural Diversity and Ethnic Minority Psychology, 14*(3), 205–214. doi:10.1037/1099-9809.14.3.205.

Yang, F. (1999). *Chinese Christians in America: Conversion, assimilation, and adhesive Iidentities.* University Park, PA: The Pennsylvania State University Press.

Chapter 5
From Walking the Thin Line Between Work and Family to Self-compassion: Working with Asian American Career Mothers

Kandice Hsu and Liang-Ying Chou

Esther's baby, Som, was a little over 4 months old when he started going to daycare. Esther, who has always been a working woman, found herself returning to work as soon as her maternity leave was up. It was quite an adjustment for both Esther and Som transitioning from homecare to daycare. Esther was feeling frustrated and guilty to send her baby to daycare at such young age due to lack of help from extended family. Although Esther has the opportunity to extend her maternity leave, financial considerations, eagerness to return to "normalcy," and the desire to complete her work project led her to the decision that it was time to return to work. Being a career mother has been fulfilling and yet stressful at times. Her story reflects many Asian American career mothers' experiences. Over the past few decades, the United States has seen both an increase in women's participation in the workforce and a rapidly growing Asian population. The nation has witnessed a significant rise in the percentage of dual-income families. More and more women have entered the labor force during the past two centuries, partly due to changes in federal legislation, educational attainment, and job opportunities (Landivar 2014).

In view of these changing demographic patterns, the increasing female presence in the workforce, and shifting societal attitudes about work and family, we (Kandice and Liang-Ying) are curious about the experiences of career mothers—women who both manage a career and raise children—in the context of Asian American families. We are both women of East Asian descent. In our personal and professional lives, we have close ties to the Asian American community and observe many Asian American women experiencing role shifts from career women to career mothers or from stay-at-home mothers to career mothers. Knowing how tough it is

K. Hsu (✉)
Orange County Health Care Agency, Santa Ana, CA, USA
e-mail: kandiceh@gmail.com

L.-Y. Chou (✉)
Private Practice, Los Angeles, CA, USA
e-mail: liangyingc@gmail.com

K.M.-T. Quek and S.-R.S. Fang (eds.), *Transition and Change in Collectivist Family Life*, AFTA SpringerBriefs in Family Therapy,
DOI 10.1007/978-3-319-50679-1_5

to be a career woman who must manage expectations associated with gender, culture values, and Western social structure, we also want to understand what it is like to be an Asian American career mother. In this chapter, we present data from a phenomenological study to challenge the traditional view on external supportive factors for career mothers, and most importantly to introduce a groundbreaking internal growth perspective that highlights the process of how career mothers create meaning to support their role as career mothers.

Traditional Views of Work and Family Among Asian American Women

The term "career mothers" refers to women who are mothers who work outside the home for an income in addition to the work they perform at home raising their children (Encyclopedia of Children's Health, n.d.). To varying degrees, all career mothers face the challenge of simultaneously juggling different, often competing roles. For instance, when a child is sick, a parent, usually the mother, stays home to take care of the child or worries about her child at work. This creates a role conflict. She must choose between prioritizing workplace demands or parental responsibilities. In Asian cultures, a collectivist orientation may influence this prioritization process, as it often emphasizes family members' obligations to one another and the support of family needs and goals over those of the individual. Familial harmony is highly valued, and it is often expected that one will sacrifice individual needs and rights for the good of the family (Quek et al. 2010).

Additionally, a hierarchical structure within Asian collectivist societies typically supports a gender-segregated division of labor, wherein women are responsible for the domestic realm and men for the work realm. Thus, these collectivist values may further burden Asian women who decide to become career mothers. According to the U.S. Department of Labor (2013), employed mothers continue to shoulder the majority of household responsibilities, rather than sharing them equally with employed fathers. As a result, role conflict experienced by Asian career mothers is likely to be heavily influenced by cultural expectations of childcare and household labor.

Existing studies (Bakker and Demerouti 2007; Lo et al. 2003) have explored the idea of work–family conflict, which is defined as a form of inter-role conflict in which pressures from the work and family domains are mutually incompatible in some aspects. Research on the topic of work–life balance has demonstrated that conflict may arise from a variety of sources (Brough et al. 2013), such as strain-based, behavior-based, and time-based, and that the relationship between work and family can be bidirectional—that is, family can interfere with work and work can interfere with family (Carlson, Kacmar, and Williams 2000). Moreover, both directions of conflict have shown to negatively impact work–family balance.

Expansionist Theory

The expansionist theory is one of the most common theories employed to understand an individual's experience with multiple roles. It states that multiple roles (for both women and men) are beneficial as reflected in their mental, physical, and relationship health (Barnett and Gareis 2006; Lee and Phillips 2006). In other words, adding the worker role is beneficial to women and adding a family role is beneficial for men. Furthermore, added income, social support, opportunities to experience success, and increased self-complexity (Barnett and Hyde 2001) are additional benefits of assuming multiple roles. For example, added income brought in by a career mother may mitigate a family's financial difficulties.

The expansionist theory stresses the importance of role quality and its part in mental, physical, and relationship health (Barnett and Hyde 2001). Role quality may be understood as the role holder's subjective experiences in a role, including perceptions of role rewards and difficulties (Cardenas et al. 2004). The perceived importance and quality of one's role may mitigate the stress related to the multiple roles of a career mother. As such, career mothers who perceive their work role as important and rewarding are more likely to better handle the demands of competing priorities of work, family, and individual lives.

Social Support

In current literature, social support is one of the most frequently discussed topics related to the experience of career mothers (Blanch and Aluja 2012; Greenhaus and Allen 2011). Social support is defined as the physical and emotional comfort given to an individual by family, friends, coworkers, and others (Pines and Zaidman 2003). It includes a sense of belonging to a community in which members love and care for one another, as well as a community that values and thinks well of the individual. Kahn and Antonucci (1980) identified three interpersonal components to social support: (a) affect—expression of liking, admiration, respect, and love, (b) affirmation—expressions of agreement or acknowledgement of the appropriateness or rightness of some act or statement of the individual and (c) aid—transactions in which direct aid or assistance is given. Unsurprisingly, career mothers who belong to strong social support networks are less likely to demonstrate burnout symptoms in their attempts to fulfill their multiple roles (Blanch and Aluja 2012).

Some research has been done regarding how career mothers manage work and family. Simon (1995) found that women reported more work-to-family conflicts than men, and attributed them to marital problems, feelings of guilt, and negative self-evaluations as parents and spouses. Studies suggest that the balancing of work and family life is more stressful for women than for men (Hammer et al. 2005; Simon 1995). However, there is a lack of understanding regarding the ways that career mothers construct and give meaning to their roles and experiences. Their process of integrating work with responsibilities within the home, and their ability to make sense of these multiple roles, have yet to be explored. In this vein, we cannot help but wonder about the meaning and essence of what it is like to be an Asian American career mother and how these meanings evolve.

Discussion in this chapter is inspired by the findings from phenomenological research. The study used in-depth qualitative interviews with ten self-identified Asian American career mothers whose ages range between 26 and 35 years old and who have at least one dependent child. Participants either were born in the United States or have lived in the United States for more than 10 years. Most of them held at least a bachelor's degree. Open-ended questions were used during the interviews to explore the meaning of being a mother, the meaning of work, and how Asian American career women attend to these commitments. Research data were collected by interviews and analyzed following Moustakas' method (Moustakas 1994). This method was chosen to best understand *what* the participants experience as career mothers and *how* they experience it. It involved transcribing the interviews and developing a list of significant statements and/or keywords that captured and described the essence of the participants' experiences as career mothers.

Building Connection Between External Resources and Internal Strengths

The stories of these Asian American career mothers disclose how they are shaped and reshaped through life influences, perceptions of careers and relationships, etc. within their social locations. Specifically, their voices reveal the importance of involving both external resources and internal strength during the journey of becoming a career mother. A creation of meaning involving both external resources and internal strengths emerges from their narratives.

Connection to External Resources

The support and connections that these Asian American women receive from their spouses, social circles, and workplace are tremendously important. These connections include: (1) teamwork between the couple in managing the needs of the family, (2) joint effort from extended family to provide physical and emotional support, (3) normalizing with friends and peers, and (4) a pro-family work culture. Together, these connections highlight both the emotional and physical support they received from relationships with different groups of people in their lives. These connections are external and made through negotiated relationships, in contrast to internal connections made with oneself, which are discussed later in this section.

Teamwork between the couple in managing the needs of the family. Among these Asian American women who view the family work as primarily their responsibility, spouses are viewed as a source of support. Teamwork between wife and husband is manifested in the division of housework and childcare. Yuki and Abby shared:

> My husband is very supportive and we have this mutual understanding. He works too and he works hard. We have the mutual understanding of "If you're really tired today but I'm not, I'll take over in taking care of the baby. Or if you're really tired, you can go to sleep and I'll clean up today." This mutual understanding is teamwork. (Yuki)

> I'm lucky that my husband helps me a lot with the kids and he cleans the house. He doesn't cook but he helps with cleaning and washing the dishes. Sometimes he helps me put out the groceries to be cooked so that when I come home from work, I can start cooking right away. Usually after we eat, he does the dishes so I can go shower and relax for a bit. (Abby)

Abby and Isabelle further illustrated the importance of dividing up childcare responsibilities using this teamwork approach

> My husband goes to work earlier than me, so he comes home earlier than me. I work later and come home later. It really works out well because when my older daughter goes to daycare, he comes home earlier so he can pick her up from school. (Abby)

> Being a mom is busy work but at least my husband is here, so he usually takes my oldest child and she would be with him. I would have my son so that is at least a 1:1 ratio so that's why it is helpful to have a supportive husband. (Isabelle)

Joint effort from extended family to provide physical and emotional support. These career mothers also discussed the importance of their extended family members, such as grandparents and siblings, in providing them with physical support, such as helping out with childcare, and providing emotional care by being supportive and having a nonjudgmental attitude toward career mothers. One mother shared that sometimes her sister took her children out for the day so that she could have a little time to herself. Also, many mothers identified that geographic proximity to grandparents aided them in childcare. Cindy shared:

> When I had my second daughter, my mom came from Vietnam to help me take care of my kids. She now lives with us. Before I had my second child, my mother-in-law was taking care of the first one while my husband and I went to work. She lives about five minutes away from us. (Cindy)

The joint effort from extended family also encompassed emotional support. Dani shared about the emotional support she received when she needed a break from caregiving. She said:

> My family is very helpful, very non-judgmental… My family is supportive. If I want to vegetate and don't want to do anything, they will still be there for me. There is no pressure from them. There is acceptance, non-judgment and support.

Normalizing with friends and peers. Many career mothers identified that normalizing the challenges of balancing work and family with their friends, colleagues, and other career mothers has been helpful to them. One mother, Beatrice, shared that "touching base with other mothers has been helpful for me… especially as a first-time mother. I felt like I could ask if what I'm experiencing with my daughter is normal." Hearing and sharing experiences with friends and peers about their utilization of maternity leave, resumption of work after delivery, duration of breastfeeding, etc. helped to relieve these young mothers' anxiety and normalize the many demands they faced. These experiences and knowledge bring comfort and connection with career mothers who share similar social locations.

Pro-family work culture. All the career mothers discussed their relationships with their employers and identified factors that were helpful as they sought to juggle multiple roles. These factors include workplace culture as well as relationships with colleagues. A pro-family work culture included benefits such as a flexible work schedule, an understanding supervisor, and a workplace that encourages family involvement. One mother remarked that her work is very flexible with time: "If something happens with my daughter in school, I can go home from work right away and my boss will be OK with that." Another shared that her flexible work schedule is one of the reasons she stayed with her company for so many years:

> They [employers] are super flexible, and that's the reason I stay too. Towards the end of my pregnancy, I took half days and they were very understanding. They are like a family. We all know each other; we've seen each other grow up and have kids, so they are very understanding and flexible. It makes a difference, like if my son is sick and I have to leave early, they don't mind. That's one of the reasons I know why my coworkers stayed too because they are so flexible with that. As long as you have everything done and [are] not slacking off, you're OK. (Yuki)

In terms of supervisory practices, having an understanding supervisor or management makes a tremendous difference:

> The management staff all has family so they are really understanding… If I need a day off, they don't ask me why. Rather, they will ask me if I'm OK, but they never question why I am not at work. You don't have to give them an explanation if you don't want to. They are just really understanding of people having a life outside of work. (Ella)

Workplaces can even encourage family involvement by hosting child-friendly events at work and having "bring your children to work" days. Grace applauded her family-oriented work environment:

> The whole organization is family friendly. The benefits are awesome. We even have this Halloween event where you can bring your children to work that day.

Connection to Internal Strengths

Learning about self. Most women from this study identified a connection to their internal strengths that helps create the narrative of who they are as career mothers. The process of finding these internal strengths occurs through a culmination of their experiences and lessons learned as they balance family and work. These internal strengths include having self-compassion, patience when adjusting to a new role, and being flexible with expectations.

Self-compassion. One of the most powerful and important internal strengths is self-compassion. Self-compassion is about extending forgiveness, acceptance, and kindness to oneself when confronted with personal failings. These sentiments highlight the relationship one builds with the self. Showing self-compassion means learning to accept one's current situation and limitations without feeling bogged down by the demands of multiple roles as a career mother. The following statements were chosen to highlight the idea of self-compassion:

> The advice I would give to a mother stepping into the role of a working mother is to have self-compassion because at the end of the day, you are the only one that understand[s] and know[s] how hard things can be with the demands and pressures. Try not to be too hard on yourself. Don't take yourself too seriously. Do meaningful things that keep you going, rest if you must, and enjoy when you can. (Dani)

> Give yourself a break. We all make mistakes and no one is perfect. I know at least with talking to a lot of moms, we are very hard on ourselves. We are probably the hardest on ourselves when it comes to things we forget to do. (Jenny)

> I would encourage them that it's OK to ask for help. It's OK to take time for yourself. There are days where you don't have to do it all, and that's something I have to remind myself [of] all the time. You don't have to be a superwoman all the time. You can ask for help and that is OK. (Fiona)

Patience when adjusting to a new role. It is important to have patience when adjusting to being a career mother. Like any adjustment phase, it requires time to adapt to the new role and responsibilities. This also means being patient with oneself and allowing oneself to experience the ups and downs of this new role. One mother shared that the adjustment to being a career mother was very difficult for her at first. She often questioned whether she could handle juggling work and being a mother. However, she reminded herself to "not be in a hurry to get back to your old routine. Take some time to enjoy being a mother. This adjustment phase is not forever. Just be patient and take your time. Everything is going to be OK."

Being flexible with expectations. Another internal strength comes from being flexible with expectations. Women said that this means being flexible with your schedule, expectations, and any changes that come along the way. For example, Yuki shared that being flexible with her own schedule helped ease her stress:

> Just pick your battles because there will be days where working and being a mom, you just have to learn to let things go. Like laundry. I always have to do laundry on Sunday, always Sunday. But once I was back to work, you realize that Monday is OK; I can do laundry on Monday too.

Another mother talked about shifting her priorities and re-organizing the family's priorities as a way to be flexible with the changing demands of raising a child. She said:

> I had a conversation with my friend and we were just chatting about going back to work and so forth, and she's having a hard time with her workplace. Her workplace was being less supportive. I told her to go over her priorities with her husband and figure out what her short-term and long-term goals are. The time with the baby is very short. Although it may seem long, it's just a phase in life. The babies grow up and it becomes another ball game. (Jenny)

Beatrice suggested that being flexible with oneself is simple: "You roll with the punches. Life happens and stuff happens and you roll with it."

Creation of Meaning Through the Interaction Between External Resources and Internal Strengths

These results highlight the significance of external resources and internal strengths. These are not two separate spheres, but rather, intersect to create a dynamic and systemically meaningful interaction between social environments and career mothers.

The career mothers interviewed exhibited great tenacity of spirit, seeking to make the best of their situations and looking for the silver lining despite challenges along the way. For example, they chose to see positive feelings of fulfillment and excitement in their work. One mother shared:

> I honestly love my job. I really do. I've been there a while so I had students that come back and to visit when they have kids. It's so rewarding to see the families and kids that made it. It makes me proud for them and also for my work as it makes a difference… Oh yeah, it's not just about money. (Yuki)

In above example, Yuki felt that the external resource (grateful clients) builds her internal strength (valuing the impact of her work) to create a meaningful experience in her career.

On the other hand, some mothers are motivated by their internal strengths. For example, Grace shared, "I want my daughter to grow up knowing that her mother was able to do it all and be successful. I want her to know that she can as well. I want to model that for her." In this example, Grace's internal strength strongly influences her self-image as a career mother and her desire that her daughter be successful like her. This internal strength helps her utilize external resources, ultimately allowing her to achieve a balance between her work and family life.

Career mothers shared that taking on a paid job also allows them to use the education they have worked so hard to earn. Some of them also expressed that they had worked prior to having children and felt like they earned their positions at work. Thus, to stay home after having children would be a waste of both the time they invested in their education and careers. Moreover, many of them expressed the importance of career as a status symbol in Asian cultures. One mother said, "Being Asian, status is really important. I want to show people that I work, I have a good job, I make good money, and I am successful." In this example, her internal strength comes from her cultural expectation, which helps her commit to both work and family.

The voices of these Asian American career mothers demonstrate the influence of external resources and internal strengths in creating a well-rounded experience of what it means to be a career mother. The creation of meanings involves a connection between social and environmental resources (external) and intrapersonal motivations, beliefs, and goals. Each aspect plays an important role in the experience of career mothers.

Going Beyond External Supportive Factors: An Internal Growth Perspective

Based on the experiences of these Asian American career mothers, we can see that integrating work and family life requires going beyond identifying and accessing external resources. Contrary to the current one-directional view of work–family life balance, which highlights the significance of supportive factors coming from external resources such as family and friends, we are able to identify a cyclical process involving an internal growth perspective.

This perspective involves a process whereby the meaning-making experiences of career mothers are created through the interaction between external resources and internal strengths. While the external resources give career mothers space to combine career goals with family aspirations, internal strengths coming from the self seek to operationalize this process. Internal strengths focus on the *self* and show how growth and empowerment can also come from within. The internal growth perspective shows that a career mother's experience is fluid because it is constantly shaped by the interactional relationship between external resources and internal strengths. Depending on how career mothers access their internal strengths and external resources, it changes their state of experience. It also highlights the active role that career mothers play in shaping their experiences by identifying internal strengths rather than relying solely on external resources (e.g., familial support, community, spirituality, etc.) to help them achieve family and work life balance.

In our study, the career mothers laid out two important components related to an internal growth perspective: learning about oneself and finding meaning in one's role as a career mother. First, learning about oneself involves having self-compassion, patience when adjusting to being a career mother, and flexibility with expectations. Many career mothers often feel like they have to be superwoman and do it all by having the perfect family and career. However, learning about oneself as a career mother requires self-compassion and giving space to oneself in order to grow and adapt. Second, the internal growth perspective is about the interactional process between external resources and internal strengths, a process that constantly shapes the career mother's experience. Figure 5.1 illustrates the cyclical process of engaging both external resources and internal strengths. This process reflects that internal strengths and external resources are equally influential to this experience. It also speaks to the fluidity of a career mother's experience, as it is continuously shaped by all the elements in the system.

The internal growth perspective suggests that internal strengths do not develop in isolation; rather, they are continuously shaped by experiences with the external world. For example, one mother shared that she realized it is OK to ask for help from her family. By acknowledging that she does not have to do it all, this mother allowed herself to turn to an external resource. In this case, her familial support reinforces her internal strength of being resourceful and knowing when and what she needs in order to help her balance family and work. With the internal growth perspective, we see a more in-depth connection between a career mother and her

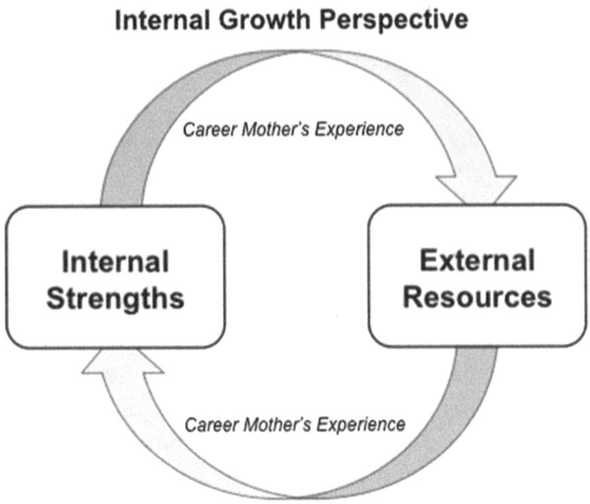

Fig. 5.1 Internal growth perspective

environment, including significant others and extended families, and how being aware of her internal processes leads to more awareness of available external resources and the utilization of these resources.

Guidelines for Clinicians: Using a Connection-Building Approach

The three messages we hope to deliver to clinicians working with career mothers are: (1) the existence of internal strengths and their influence on career mothers' experiences, (2) the interactional relationship between external resources and internal strengths, and (3) recognizing and challenging societal idea that parenting is a woman's job. We hope that clinicians will help career mothers develop the "self-of-a-career-mother" by creating empowering meaning that is inclusive of their work, family, and self. The phrase "self-of-a-career-mother" is a modification of the term "self-of-a-therapist." Similar to the understanding of "self-of-a-therapist," self-of-a-career-mother promotes one's inner process—accepting what is, knowing oneself, and looking at possibilities (Lum 2002). To do so, we recommend clinicians consider a connection-building approach that is based on the internal growth perspective discussed previously to help career mothers get in touch with their internal strengths and activate the cyclical process of engaging both internal strengths and external resources. The following are some pointers that can help clinicians engage the internal growth perspective:

- Facilitate discussion with the client to explore one particular experience in which she was aware of the relationship between internal strength and external resources.

- Explore the client's external resources such as faith community, friends, and extended families and then discuss how these have reinforced an internal strength.
- Involve fathers in co-parenting as this process can positively impact on client's inner strengths.
- Help clients create a work/family narrative that sees parenting beyond a woman's job while involving self-compassion when faced with challenges.

Clinically, we promote working with Asian American career mothers from a circular process wherein a discussion of external resources as well as the involvement of significant others and extended families becomes routine in the meaning-making process. We would also like to encourage all clinicians working with this population to take an advocacy role and challenge the societal discourse of parenting as a woman's job by encouraging significant others, spouses, and extended family to be accountable for their role in shifting this societal discourse. As career mothers learn to advocate for themselves and engage with external resources, it allows them to further develop their connections to internal strengths and solidify self-empowerment. In other words, based on the internal growth perspective, a client's ability to self-advocate serves as an indicator that symbolizes her integration of internal strengths and external resources, as well as reveals the nurturing and engaging nature of her environment in which family work is shared responsibility among family members.

References

Bakker, A. B., & Demerouti, E. (2007). The job demands–resources model: State of the art. *Journal of Managerial Psychology, 22,* 309–328.

Barnett, R. C., & Gareis, K. C. (2006). Role Theory Perspectives on Work and Family. In M. Pitt-Catsouphes, E. E. Kossek, S. Sweet, M. Pitt-Catsouphes, E. E. Kossek, & S. Sweet (Eds.), *The work and family handbook: Multi-disciplinary perspectives, methods, and approaches* (pp. 209–221). Mahwah, NJ, US: Lawrence Erlbaum Associates Publishers.

Barnett, R. C., & Hyde, J. S. (2001). Women, men, work, and family: An expansionist theory. *American Psychologist, 56,* 781–796. doi:10.1037//0003-066X.56.10.781.

Blanch, A., & Aluja, A. (2012). Social support (family and supervisor), work–family conflict, and burnout: Sex differences. *Human Relations, 65*(7), 811–833. doi:10.1177/0018726712440471.

Brough, P., Timms, C., Siu, O., Kalliath, T., O'Driscoll, M. P., & Sit, C. H. P. (2013). Validation of the job demands–resources model in cross-national samples: Cross-sectional and longitudinal predictions of psychological strain and work engagement. *Human Relations, 66,* 1311–1335.

Cardenas, R. A., Major, D. A., & Bernas, K. H. (2004). Exploring work and family distractions: Antecedents and Outcomes. *International Journal of Stress Management, 11,* 346–365. doi:10.1037/1072-5245.11.4.346.

Carlson, D. S., Kacmar, K. M., & Williams, L. J. (2000). Construction and initial validation of a multidemensional measure of work-family conflict. *Journal of Vocational Behavior, 56,* 249–276.

Working Mothers. (n.d.). In *Encyclopedia of Children's Health.* Retrieved from http://www.healthofchildren.com/U-Z/Working-Mothers.html.
Hammer, L. B., Newsom, J. T., Brockwood, K. J., & Colton, C. L. (2005). A longitudinal study of the effects of dual-earner couples' utilization of family-friendly workplace supports on work and family outcomes. *Journal of Applied Psychology, 90*(4), 799–810. doi:10.1037/0021-9010.90.4.799.
Kahn, R. L., & Antonucci, T. C. (1980). Convoys over the life course: attachments, roles, and social support. In P. B. Baltes & O. G. Brim Jr. (Eds.), *Life-span Development and Behavior* (pp. 253–286). New York: Academic Press.
Greenhaus, J. H, & Allen, T. D. (2011). Work-family balance: A review and extension of the literature. In J. C. Quick, & L. E. Tetrick (Eds.), *Handbook of occupational health psychology* (vol. *2,* pp. 165–183). Washington, DC: American Psychological Association
Landivar, L. C. (2014). Opting out, scaling back, or business-as-usual? An occupational assessment of women's employment. *Sociology Forum, 29,* 189–214. doi:10.1111/socf.12075.
Lee, J. A., & Phillips, S. J. (2006). Work and family: Can you have it all? *The Psychologist Manager Journal, 9*(1), 41–57. doi:10.1207/s15503461tpmj0901_5.
Lo, S., Stone, R., & Ng, C. W. (2003). Work-family conflict and coping strategies adopted by female married professionals in Hong Kong. *Women in Management Review, 18,* 182–190.
Lum, W. (2002). The use of self of the therapist. *Contemporary Family Therapy, 24,* 181–197.
Moustakas, C. (1994). *Phenomenological research methods.* Thousand Oaks, CA: Sage.
Pines, A. M., & Zaidman, N. (2003). Gender, culture, and social support: A male-female, Israeli Jewish-Arab comparison. *Sex Roles, 49,* 571–586.
Quek, K., Knudson-Martin, C., Rue, D., & Alabiso, C. (2010). Relational Harmony: A New Model of Collectivism and Gender Equality among Asian American Couples. *Journal of Family Issues (Special Edition on Asian American Families), 31,* 358–380.
Simon, R. W. (1995). Gender, multiple roles, role meaning, and mental health. *Journal of Health and Social Behavior, 36,* 182–194.
United States Department of Labor (2013). *Women in the labor force: A databook.* Retrieved from http://www.dol.gov/wb/stats/stats_data.htm.

Chapter 6
The Role of Chinese Grandparents in Their Adult Children's Parenting Practices in the United States

Hao-Min Chen and Denise C. Lewis

More than 2.5 million grandparents are taking on the role of parents in the United States. Because of various factors, such as parental death, substance abuse, incarceration, mental health issues, military deployment, teen pregnancy, abandonment, abuse, or neglect, these grandparents provide primary care for their grandchildren (Facciolo 2012). Previous studies have reported that grandparents, including Chinese grandparents, contribute to cooking, shopping, housekeeping, and caring for grandchildren in their households, and that some grandparents experience stress due to the extensiveness of these responsibilities (Goh and Kuczynski 2010). However, there are few studies exploring more deeply these areas of Chinese grandparents' lives. The limited information available about Chinese multigenerational households in the U.S. and their unique family dynamics creates challenges for mental health professionals seeking effective engagement with these families. We aim to respond to the needs of the field by exploring cultural and contextual backgrounds surrounding intergenerational relationships and Chinese grandparents' involvement in their adult children's parenting practices in the United States.

Hao-Min Chen is an international faculty member and therapist originally from Taiwan. She believes that family relationships are socially constructed and are shaped by cultural contexts. Thus, she pays attention to socially constructed power associated with ethnic norms when studying Chinese grandparents in the United

---

This chapter is a revised version of Chen and Lewis (2015). Chinese grandparents' involvement in their adult children's parenting practices in the United States. Contemporary Family Therapy, DOI:10.1007/s10591-014-9321-7.

H.-M. Chen (✉)
Couple and Family Therapy Program, Alliant International University, Irvine, CA, USA
e-mail: hmchen@alliant.edu

D.C. Lewis
College of Family and Consumer Sciences, University of Georgia, Athens, GA, USA

K.M.-T. Quek and S.-R.S. Fang (eds.), *Transition and Change in Collectivist Family Life*, AFTA SpringerBriefs in Family Therapy,
DOI 10.1007/978-3-319-50679-1_6

States. Denise Lewis is of Euro-American heritage and is a cross-cultural family gerontologist with many years of experience studying intergenerational relations. She has particular interest in the ways families interpret responsibilities and provide care, and how shifts in sociocultural understandings are navigated within and across generations. In this chapter, we strive to create space for the voices of those living in Chinese multigenerational households in the United States and explore the politics of diverse social locations.

Grandparents, Parents, and Grandchildren

Grandparents in China contribute to their adult children's households by cooking, shopping, housekeeping, and caring for grandchildren (Goh and Kuczynski 2010). Goh (2006) found that grandparents in South China experienced childcare as mentally and physically exhausting. Similarly, a cross-sectional comparative pilot study conducted in Taiwan found that 55.6% of Chinese grandparent caregivers reported psychological distress, even though 86.7% of these grandparents received caregiving support from other family members (Lo and Liu 2009). Despite these statistics, some theorists indirectly suggest that engaging with a younger generation can be a positive experience, as it might provide a sense of meaning for the grandparents in their later stages of life (Byers et al. 2008). Studies in Taiwan confirmed this hypothesis, reporting that grandparent caregivers were more likely to have better self-rated health, higher life satisfaction, and fewer depressive symptoms (Ku et al. 2013). In any case, findings based on research in Asian countries (e.g., Goh and Kuczynski 2010) do not necessarily reflect the experiences of Chinese families and grandparents in the United States.

Chinese grandparents' level of involvement in their adult children's parenting practices in the United States has not been adequately explored (Nagata et al. 2010). Studies on U.S. populations of Chinese grandparents focus on direct caregiving from grandparents to their grandchildren (Nagata et al. 2010). Additionally, Nagata et al. (2010) note that Chinese grandparents living in the United States are often confronted with unique challenges, such as employment, immigration/visa issues, changes in environments and lifestyles, and the possibility of dependency on their adult children or grandchildren (Nagata et al. 2010). They have not addressed Chinese grandparents' relationships with their adult children and their roles in multigenerational households in the United States.

Grandparents exert influence on familial and parental systems (i.e., grandparent-parent subsystem), which impacts their adult children's parenting practices. Many Chinese grandparents in the United States provide indirect parenting support or direct caregiving to their grandchildren (Yoon 2005). Younger, able-bodied grandmothers are more likely than comparable grandfathers to give care to their grandchildren. Consistent with their cultural values, grandparents in the United States focus on their grandchildren's moral character development, manners, and achievements.

Chinese Families in a Changing Society

The historical and cultural backgrounds of Chinese societies have influenced Chinese families living in China, Taiwan, and the United States. The Communist takeover of China, the one-child policy, the Cultural Revolution, and changes in the economic growth of China have created major social, economic, and political changes throughout Chinese societies across Mainland China, Taiwan, and the United States. Changes in Chinese familial relationships in the United States include the erosion of traditional roles, power shifts across generations, and discordant interpretations of filial piety. Both older and younger generations challenge and redefine traditions and are exploring new roles.

Family structure and power shift. The one-child family planning policy, initiated in the 1980s and ended in 2015, is a population control program of the Chinese government. Beginning in the 2000s, the government began to allow more exceptions to this policy for parents who are ethnic minorities or for situations in which both parents are themselves each an only child. Consequently, the one-child policy has made a substantial impact on Chinese family hierarchy. Prior to the implementation of the policy, grandparents were viewed through a traditional Confucianism lens (Lee and Mock 2005) as authority figures in the family and were the ultimate experts on parenting and raising children (Chuang 2009). The policy-dictated four-two-one structure (four grandparents, two parents, one child) has effectively prolonged parental indulgence and promoted a more Westernized child-centered parenting approach, especially in well-educated families (Chuang 2009). Autonomy of parents and grandchildren has increased, and this shift of hierarchy and relational power has created power struggles between older and younger generations when dealing with differences in parenting.

Changing interpretation and the practice of filial piety. The principle of filial piety is greatly cherished in traditional Chinese culture. Adult children are expected to provide care for their older parents (Chuang 2009). Some Chinese adults in the United States, however, do not feel responsible for the care of their older parents. Thanks to improvement of the overall economic environment in their countries of origin, many aging parents are now able to support themselves financially rather than relyling on their adult children. In addition, adult children are influenced by Western individualistic ideas of family practices and no longer consider providing care for their parents an obligation. Although filial piety and family connections are still emphasized, actual practices of filial piety have become more diverse and personalized in the United States. This means that adult children may show their appreciation and respect for their older parents in nontraditional ways, such as through phone calls or gifts rather than visits (van Willigen and Lewis 2006). Factors such as an individual's gender, self-reported health, availability of other family members, his or her familial relationships, and overall familial and relational history influence who is providing care to elderly parents. Chinese grandparents, though, continue to offer assistance to their adult children's households and view it as a way to enjoy family happiness, maintain emotional closeness, and nurture a stronger sense of filial obligation in the family. Most Chinese grandparents in the United States report a noninterference rather than a directive style of engagement as grandparents, a departure from the traditional pattern that is based on strong hierarchical traditions (Nagata et al. 2010).

This chapter explores contemporary Chinese family dynamics between grandparents and their adult children in the United States. Our findings are based on interviews with nine Chinese families residing in the United States. Families' stories surrounding their perceived changes in power dynamics, intergenerational relationships, and boundaries across individualism and independence are explored. Furthermore, by adopting the concept of grandparents' "involvement" and "family-defined" parenting participation, we show how Chinese families interact when viewed through a culturally responsive lens. This lens provides insights into the collision of collectivism and individualistic traditions associated with families in the United States.

Method

The epistomological, theoretical, and methodological foundations of this study are found in social constructionism, narrative theory, and ethnography. We conducted semi-structured interviews using open-ended questions with Chinese grandparents and their adult children who were originally from Mainland China (7 families) or Taiwan (2 families) and who lived in a southern region of the United States. Each family consisted of members from three generations (i.e., at least one grandparent, one parent, and one grandchild). Grandparents and parents were interviewed separately, using each participant's choice of Mandarin or English. Participants' acculturation levels varied. In general, parents were more acculturated than grandparents. Some grandparents spoke fluent English and were familiar with American customs, food, and ways of living, while others barely spoke any English and socialized only with people who spoke the same language. Analysis followed a pathway of open coding, focused coding, thematic development, and conceptually clustered matrices.

Parenting and Grand-parenting Involvement

Stories from both generations describe the grandparents' types and degree of involvement in their adult children's parenting practices. Family stories often begin with the younger parents' needs for childcare and household assistance in the United States. Extended family members, including grandparents from the other parent's side, discuss ways to fulfill the adult children's childcare needs and determine types of involvement in supportive practices. Influences of culture of origin, familial relationships, and local communities are found in family members' narratives.

How Did the Grandparents Get Here?

Most of the Chinese parents are first-generation or 1.5-generation immigrants, young professionals, and full-time workers. They spoke English well and were familiar with American ways of living. However, they juggle job demands, childcare, and adjustment to a foreign country, and are in need of someone trustworthy to help with household chores, childcare, and emotional support and decision-making. One father (Li) said that he works full time and that "operating under another language is challenging... When I get home, I am exhausted and don't have any energy left for a crying child or a full load of dirty laundry. My wife and I [could] really use some help from my mom." Many parents prefer someone in the family who understands Chinese culture and who values family. They view assistance from grandparents as economical, trustworthy, and, more importantly, culturally and linguistically appropriate. Parents mention that their children learn Chinese languages (e.g., Mandarin or other dialects) and cultural norms from grandparents. Moreover, involving grandparents creates more family time and strengthens closeness among family members.

The four-two-one family structure of China that focuses more on the younger generation's needs often facilitates a negotiation process for answering younger parents' requests for help from the older generation. Modern families from Taiwan with one or two children have shared this tendency too. Often grandparents from both the mother's and father's sides expressed their willingness to help. This is consistent with the work by Shwalb et al. (2004) and Chuang (2009). A collective negotiation ensued and it established who, and in what order, grandparents would travel to the United States to provide help to their adult children. Similar to findings by Nagata et al. (2010), this decision depends on the health condition, work demands, and residential areas of the grandparents. An additional complication can arise because of limits on the length of time a grandparent may legally remain in the United States due to visa restrictions. Grandparents often chose to take turns so they could both respect the legal limits of their stay and extend and maximize the support they provide to their children's generation.

Grandparents' Involvement in Parenting Practices

Both grandparents' and their adult children's narratives revealed a great level of positive and supportive grandparent involvement in parenting practices in the United States. No one described grandparents' involvement as negative or interfering. However, the forms of parenting involvement varied from family to family.

Due to the various contextual and societal shifts, Chinese families residing in the United States are deviating slowly from traditional social norms. Instead of following these traditional expectations, such as a more rigid practice of filial piety and the assumption that grandparents hold absolute power when it comes to raising the grandchildren, families now formulate different definitions about the "right amount" of parenting participation from grandparents. The right amount can include offering direct childcare to the grandchildren, emotional support and decision-making aid to the younger parents, meal preparation, and chore assistance to the whole family. These findings confirm systemic assumptions of nonlinear relationships between family members, and they imply multiple (direct and indirect) ways of connecting and providing support. Chinese grandparents do not only provide direct care to the grandchildren but also support the parenting systems (i.e., the younger parents) and their families as whole units. One mother, Sun, described multiple ways her mother helped support her and her growing family. She said:

> There is a lot housework you have to do every day. My mom gets up 6 o'clock every morning and makes breakfast for us. After that she dresses my daughter for school when I do my yoga of the day… When I am out for work, she does the laundry, cleans the house, and prepares for dinner… When my daughter gets home, she plays with her and takes her out for a walk. After that, she bathes my daughter and feeds her….

Most grandparents offered help within but not outside their households. For example, they wash laundry but rarely talk to their grandchildren's teachers. Possibly because of language difficulties or unfamiliarity with the local systems, grandparents tend to not interact with personnel from their grandchildren's school systems or medical providers. In addition, when interacting with grandchildren, most grandparents demonstrate a nondirective style, which differs from traditional values that focus on grandparents' absolute power in the household, (Nagata et al. 2010). For example, Grandmother Zhao deferred to the parents' authority and said, "They are the parents. They have the responsibilities to teach them [the grandchildren] and to discipline. We are the grandparents. We play with them." Grandmother Chou made a similar point, saying, "I would be crossing the line if I discipline [my grandson]. She [the parent] is the mother. It is her responsibility." Grandparents respect the parenting decisions their adult children make and only give advice when asked. They express their opinions openly but refrain from enforcing them. Grandmother Feng noted this change from traditional elder-centric intergenerational relationships. She said, "The time is so different. Things are different from where I was raised. My daughter grows up here and knows more about the system… She went to college here. She has her own way of parenting, a more Americanized way." Like her, other Chinese grandparents view the difference between generations regarding parenting as associated with changes across time and the influence of Western individualism and education.

Grandparents often talk about various issues encountered by their adult children and offer listening, empathy, and insights. Topics discussed include parenting differences in Mainland China, Taiwan, and the United States, across both generational and cultural axes. Their conversations also include daily life challenges, such as difficulty finding a job, places to eat authentic Asian food, or how to buy a good house in a nice school district. The actions of the grandparents, such as food preparation and helping with house chores, are instrumentally supportive, while conversations are emotionally supportive of the young couples' decision-making. The combination of instrumental and emotional support from the grandparents to the parents relieves some of the cultural and environmental stress felt by the adult children. It also indirectly improves adult children's parenting practices in the United States.

Instrumental and emotional assistance given from the older generation to the younger generation is counter to the traditional practice of filial piety, in which younger family members serve and provide emotional and instrumental support to their elders. However, many young couples feel comfortable with their older parents' assistance and are appreciative of them. They make efforts to repay or reward their older parents with sightseeing or shopping, making sure they feel cared for and valued in return. Father Wang described how he and his wife recognized the sacrifice of his mother and compensated her efforts by taking her out for sightseeing trips. He said, "It was not easy for her to make it here," and he wanted to show his gratitude. Similarly, Mother Chien shared, "I got my father-in-law some electronic devices he likes. I took him out for shopping and we compared product details and prices together. I always seek to get something he likes."

Coping as a family in a foreign country. Grandparents and their adult children constantly emphasize the value of family togetherness and highlight the strengths of each family member. Instead of focusing on their stresses and problems, they chose to underscore their daily life coping strategies as individuals (grandparents and parents) and as a collective family. Childcare and household assistance needs of the younger parents are often viewed as family issues instead of individual issues. Grandfather Zhao exemplifies how the collectivist view overshadows individual needs. He said of his son, "He [the adult child] needs me and I am here." Both grandparents and parents cherish the contributions they make to one another, with parents attributing their parenting success or their children's achievements directly to the grandparents' involvement. One mother (Chien) described the role her mother played in her young daughter's success:

> Our life here is hard. We need a lot of help. That is why my mom is here. We are so happy that she is here. Yu [my daughter] won a painting trophy last month. It is because of my mom's help that Yu and I can survive here.

Family togetherness is also communicated through food. In many Chinese families, food is a way to connect with one another. By preparing and sharing food, grandparents show their love and support for the younger couples in a nonverbal, sacrificial way. Mother Chien described her family relationship using food as a metaphor for closeness:

> My in-laws devoted all of their hearts and efforts to my husband. Chinese parents are like that. If there was only one thing left to eat in the household, they would give the food to the child even though he/she is an adult now... Their family survived poverty but every time when I visit their house, they offer me the best food they have instead of eating it themselves.

Similarly, Grandmother Sun said in a soft voice with tears in her eyes, "As long as he likes the food I cook. I will cook for him forever." Her love for her adult child and her grandchildren was well served in each dish she made.

As mentioned previously, grandparents and parents in this study embrace an overall optimistic perspective and choose to focus on positive segments of engagement. They rarely complain about their problems and stressors, instead focusing on their strengths and their daily life coping strategies as individuals (grandparents and parents) and as a collective family unit. Their stories about challenges and how they overcome those challenges with effective family-centered coping strategies reflect a cultural value of family cohesiveness carried through to the next generation.

In summary, many Chinese grandparents play a supportive role in their adult children's parenting practices and provide household assistance in the United States. Grandparents contribute to these multigenerational households by offering direct childcare to the grandchildren, emotional support and decision-making aid to the younger parents, or meal preparation and chore assistance to the whole family. However, as mentioned earlier, the "right amount" of this grandparental involvement is often negotiated among the family members and may vary widely from family to family.

Recommendations for Therapists

A systemic and strengths-based approach is recommended when working with a Chinese population involving grandparents, adult children, and their offspring. Specifically, we recommend that therapists focus on relationally appropriate practices. Since a more family-involved lifestyle is expected in Chinese families, it could be relationally appropriate to acknowledge intergenerational relationships by inviting grandparents to sessions to better understand a Chinese family's relationship dynamics. Conversations with grandparents may give therapists more information about the needs and challenges of the younger parents, as well as provide the younger parents with insights about how to best acknowledge their parents' participation and influence on their own parenting practices.

Cultural strengths provided by grandparents, similar to recommendations made by Lee and Mock (2005) that address family members' perceptions of social changes, and how these cultural strengths and social changes influence intergenerational relationships, should be explored. Sample questions include: "What support do you receive from extended family members? Do you think it is the 'right amount'? Why or why not?" "How does the economic change in China affect our family in the United States?" "Do you think the economic change or one-child policy influence how you parent your child/grandchild? Why or why not? What are the influences?" However, when discussing the modern grandparents' role and involvement in their adult children's parenting, therapists must avoid preconceptions or automatic imposition of static viewpoints. For instance, therapists should not assume that every Chinese grandparent is happy to raise his or her grandchild, or that all families are equally impacted by the social changes discussed herein or respond to those changes in the same ways.

Focusing on the value of family and interpersonal harmony as a function and goal of therapy could be achieved by inviting each family member to talk about his or her views and perceptions of the cultural expectations for grandparents and parents. It is equally important that therapists do not assume that every Chinese family is under the same influence of these philosophical traditions emphasizing harmony in interpersonal relationships. Moreover, to better serve this generation of grandparents, we recommend mental health agencies actively seek out multilingual therapists. Most Chinese grandparents whose first language is not English prefer therapists who speak their language, such as Mandarin, Cantonese, or other dialects.

Finally, we suggest therapists remain attuned to the delivery of caring, understanding, and empathy in each session. Particularly, when engaging grandparents, basic attending skills such nodding, smiling, and summarizing should be used liberally. Therapists should consider a systemic view in order to be culturally appropriate for comprehending different layers of interactions between family subsystems (e.g., grandparents and parents, parents and grandchildren, grandparents and grandchildren). Clinicians are encouraged to explore both individual stories and relational and collective family narratives regarding parenting. We caution, however, that grandparents and parents from Mainland China and Taiwan are a heterogeneous group. Knowledge presented in this chapter can serve as scaffolding to therapists' understanding of the general culture. Therapists should always be aware of the individual differences associated with geographical locations, historical events, and environmental variances.

References

Byers, A. L., Levy, B. R., Allore, H. G., Bruce, M. L., & Kasl, S. V. (2008). When parents matter to their adult children: Filial reliance associated with parents' depressive symptoms. *Journals of Gerontology Series B, Psychological Sciences and Social Sciences*, 63B(1), 33–40.

Chuang, S. S. (2009). Transformation and change: parenting in Chinese societies. In J. A. Mancini & K. A. Roberto (Eds.), *Pathways of human development: Explorations of change*. Lanham: Lexington Books.

Facciolo, C. (2012). More than 2.5 million grandparents take on role of parent. *USA Today News*. Retrieved from http://usatoday30.usatoday.com/news/health/wellness/story/2012-04-12/rise-of-granparents-grandfamilies/54206854/1.

Goh, E. C. L. (2006). Raising the precious single child in urban China—An intergenerational joint mission between parents and grandparents. *Journal of Intergenerational Relationships, 4*(3), 7–28.

Goh, E. C. L., & Kuczynski, L. (2010). Only Children and their coalition of parents: Considering grandparents and parents as joint caregivers in urban Xiamen, China. *Asian Journal of Social Psychology, 13*(4), 221–231.

Ku, L. E., Stearns, S. C., Van Houtven, C. H., Lee, S. D., Dilworth-Anderson, P., & Konrad, T. R. (2013). Impact of caring for grandchildren on the health of grandparents in Taiwan. *Journal of Gerontology*. doi:10.1093/geronb/gbt090.

Lee, E., & Mock, M. R. (2005). Chinese Families. In M. McGoldrick, J. Giordano, & N. Garcia-Preto (Eds.), *Ethnicity and family therapy* (3rd ed.). New York, NY: Guilford Press.

Lo, M., & Liu, Y.-H. (2009). Quality of life among older grandparent caregivers: A pilot study. *Journal of Advanced Nursing, 65*(7), 1475–1484. doi:10.1111/j.1365-2648.2009.05000.x.

Nagata, D. K., Cheng, W. J. Y., & Tsai-Chae, A. H. (2010). Chinese American grandmothering: A qualitative exploration. *Asian American Journal of Psychology, 1*(2), 151–161. doi:10.1037/a0019963.

Shwalb, D. W., Nakazawa, J., Yamamoto, T., & Hyun, J.-H. (2004). Fathering in Japanese, Chinese, and Korean cultures: A review of the research literature. In M. E. Lamb (Ed.), *The role of the father in child development* (4th ed., pp. 146–181). Hoboken, NJ: Wiley

van Willigen, J., & Lewis, D. C. (2006). Culture as the context of aging. In H. Yoon & J. Hendricks (Eds.), *Handbook of Asian Aging* (pp. 117–141). Amityville, NY: Baywood Publishing Company.

Yoon, S. M. (2005). Characteristics and needs of Asian-American grandparent caregivers: A study of Chinese-American and Korean-American grandparents in New York City. *Journal of Gerontological Social Work, 44*(3–4), 75–94.

Chapter 7
Balancing the Old and the New: The Case of Second-Generation Filipino American Women

Jennifer L. Del-Mundo and Karen Mui-Teng Quek

Second-generation Filipino American women face the stressful task of managing the influences of two cultures, balancing the conflicting expectations and values of Filipino culture and American culture simultaneously (Salam 2005). Finding a balance between being "too ethnic" in the eyes of the dominant culture and being "too American" in the eyes of their families and wider ethnic group can be difficult and frustrating, impacting adjustment processes and identity development (Espiritu and Wolf 2001; Nadal 2011).

The issue of identity among second-generation Filipino American women can be better understood when examined from a historical perspective that considers the relationship between the Philippines and the United States (Zhou and Xiong 2005). Although the Philippines is considered part of the continent of Asia, Filipinos are perhaps more dissimilar than similar to other Asian groups and cultures in a variety of ways due to a long history of colonization by Spain and later by the United States. Tuason et al. (2007) suggest that Filipinos are an atypical Asian subgroup with variations within the culture that include differing values, traditions, language, and physical appearance.

Beginning in the 1900s, Filipinos came to the United States in several waves to study, work, and serve in the military. Despite often working in menial and labor-intensive positions, Filipinos continued to glorify life in the United States (Espiritu 1995). The Philippines was a U.S. colony for about fifty years, and consequently, many Filipinos and Filipino Americans developed a colonial mentality, viewing themselves as "less than" relative to the dominant white American group (David 2008). Researchers argued that this colonial mentality is common for many Filipinos and negatively impacts their ethnic identity and ultimately, their

J.L. Del-Mundo
Private Practice, Irvine, CA, USA

K.M.-T. Quek (✉)
Marriage and Family Therapy Program, Bethel University, San Diego, CA, USA
e-mail: karen-quek@bethel.edu

K.M.-T. Quek and S.-R.S. Fang (eds.), *Transition and Change in Collectivist Family Life*, AFTA SpringerBriefs in Family Therapy,
DOI 10.1007/978-3-319-50679-1_7

mental health (David and Okazaki 2006). Relatedly, the history of Filipino immigration to the United States is embedded with incidents of discrimination. This discrimination, and the associated devaluation of Filipino culture, has important implications for current Filipino American women and how they perceive themselves and their culture (Espiritu and Wolf 2001).

Second-Generation Filipino American Women

Literature regarding the position of Filipino American women in society is conflicting. Women's gender roles are described as either egalitarian or patriarchal (Agbayani-Siewert and Jones 1997). This may be due to the fact that prior to Spanish occupation of the Philippines, Filipino culture and society were matrilineal. However, after Spanish influence took hold of Filipino natives, concepts related to machismo and the patriarchal religion of Catholicism were incorporated into Filipino culture (Enrile and Agbayani 2007).

Family role expectations continue to be confusing and challenging for Filipino American women because successful first-generation Filipino female workers who migrated overseas tend to enact gendered scripts prevalent in the Philippines (Paul 2015). As these female migrants continue their traditional supporting duties as daughters, wives, sisters and/or mothers, their gender-role modeling has created an expectation for daughters to behave according to more conservative gender roles (Enrile and Agbayani 2007).

Therefore, it is important to understand the experience of women of Filipino descent, as their intersecting gender and cultural contexts can potentially influence their interpretation of gender and ethnic identity and their understanding of roles in varying ways (Heras 2007). In this chapter, we (Jennifer and Karen) aim to understand how second-generation Filipina Americans' views of women and gender roles affect their identity construction. Jennifer is a second-generation Filipino American woman who finds it difficult to strike a balance between both cultures, specifically, the Filipino culture of her home life and the American culture of her social life. Karen is Singapore-born Chinese woman who teaches in a couple and family therapy program in the United States. This chapter is based on Jennifer's original study that Karen supervised.

Study Design

We used a qualitative phenomenological design to allow the women to share their contemporary and lived experiences related to adjustment and perceptions of self and ethnicity, as well as stories of marginalization that may impact their overall sense of who they are and the world they live in. All 19 American-born Filipinas were born in Southern California. Their ages ranged between 18 and 35 years old with an average of 27 years. Twelve were married. Of the 19 participants, three were in college, one held an associate's degree, 13 had bachelor's degrees, and two had master's degrees. Those who worked held white-collar jobs. Only two of the participants were able to speak Tagalog in addition to English. All of the participants' parents immigrated to the United States between the 1960s and the 1980s.

Conflict in Gender Roles and Identity

All second-generation Filipino American women in this study experienced gender marginalization. They seemed to receive the shorter end of the stick in life because they were not spared from second-class treatment based on their status as females. Many expectations were imposed on them. Their stories describe dissonance around gender roles and identity. On one hand, they were expected to fulfill traditional gender roles, such as having a family, being obedient to their parents, and completing domestic tasks. On the other hand, they were to simultaneously fulfill contemporary Western female roles, such as obtaining a good education, having a successful career, and making money. One of the participants, Kathleen, summed up the general sentiment: "You don't date anyone until you finish school. You don't have sex until you're married. Everything has to be in perfect order: school, then boyfriend, then you get married, then have kids."

Traditional Gendered Female Roles

Even though other researchers have suggested that Filipino Americans held both egalitarian and conservative attitudes toward gender roles (Agbayani-Siewert 2004; Enrile and Agbayani 2007), nearly all participants reported that they were expected to provide attention associated with their gendered responsibilities, i.e., accepting a domestic role as their central identity. It seems that holding an egalitarian attitude is not tantamount to practical gender equality in their day-to-day responsibilities. Almost all women identified "making family your top priority" as an important expectation in Filipino culture. Many of them were raised in close-knit families and had a sense of duty to them. Parents instill the message that as adults, women are expected to extend this sense of duty to their own families and extended families.

Family matters: The imperatives of the gender structure largely determine that women are the custodians of family relationships (Philpot et al. 1997). In other words, women are strongly socialized to prioritize relationships and tend to organize their lives around family social events. Many participants remembered their parents requiring them to have meals together as a family every night. During these times, no one was supposed to focus on anything else except interacting with one another. Katie stated "You're supposed to be spending time, like talking about your day. It's really important to wait for each other, even if someone comes home late."

Danielle had a similar experience and remembered that she would even have to refuse going out with friends or social events if it interfered with her family's mealtimes. They learned these lessons at a young age. Emily's interactions with her family extended beyond mealtimes. She remembered having large family parties nearly every weekend. Family gatherings seemed boisterous, as she recalled people drinking, playing mahjong and poker, and listening to music. Regarding the family relations, she states:

> Growing up, no matter what age… I'm always doing things with family. I'm always choosing to do things with family, like celebrate my birthday with my family… I'm always hanging out with my mom.

As part of the expectation that they will be the custodians of family relationships, women are expected to care for and respect their parents or elders. Maria stated that respect for elders is an important Filipino value. For example, younger Filipinos are expected to bow and touch their forehead to the back of an elder's hand. This ritual, called *mano po*, expresses respect for the elder, asks for the elder's blessing, and honors the elder's wisdom and life experience. Besides providing care for elderly family members, Faith noticed that Filipinos expect younger Filipinas to exhibit respect toward any Filipino who is older than them. One way younger members of the Filipino community convey this respect is by utilizing terms such as *manang* (older sister), *manong* (older brother), *ate* (older sister), or *kuya* (older brother). On the one hand, United States-born Filipino women seem to be returning to the core cultural values of their parents and they "do not follow the typical acculturation framework wherein the longer a group is in the host country the more acculturated they become" (Ernile and Agbayani 2007, p.1). On the other hand, as young Filipino females, their experiences are not independent of social positions like age, culture, and gender. In fact, intersection between age and gender within the Filipino cultural context places these participants as social capital to perpetuate and maintain their cultural norms. Even though they embody traditional ideals and behaviors, social networks of respecting and caring people add to quality of life and familial bonding.

Be pretty and marry a good husband: Filipino American women have been raised to embrace a strong sense of obligation to their immediate families. One familial expectation is to be beautiful and be married, as their identity depends on whether they can get married and whether they can have children. Therefore, they report pressure to maintain their appearances well so that they can attract a husband and subsequently start their own families. Growing up, Faith recalled how she was often criticized and reprimanded if she did not keep up her appearance. She states

> So there's a concern if I get injured… as a result of getting injured, my physical appearance would be diminished in some form. Any time I fell over and got a scar, I was criticized. I needed to maintain a certain level of beauty in order to find a man. Pretty simple. As a teenager, I had acne. My uncles would rub my forehead and say, "It's like sandpaper."… Aunties who came to visit… the first words out of their mouths, "Oh my God! Look at you now. You're so fat… Do you never stop eating?… *Tabachoy na*! (She's a fatty now!)"

Likewise, Emily shared that her aunt, who is a celebrity and actress in the Philippines, often gives her advice about beauty. Emily, who prided herself on her athleticism, stated her aunt would tell her, "You look really good, but don't forget that men like their women soft… Be fit but not too fit because a guy likes his woman feminine."

Many of the participants were in agreement regarding which physical features are usually associated with being Filipino: dark skin, almond-shaped eyes, short stature, flat noses, and dark hair. Although these features simply describe the general appearance of Filipinas, the participants seemed to equate these features with unattractiveness. As a result, Samantha, Emily, and Sharon perceived themselves as less powerful and less influential because they viewed their appearances as less attractive. They have absorbed subtle gender messages through various socializing agents such as their parents and extended families.

Samantha shared that at the age of 4 or 5 years old, she remembered feeling disappointed about her appearance: "I remembered being upset that I wasn't blonde… I had Barbie dolls with blonde hair, so I thought I was blonde." She recalled feeling confused and angry in that moment. Currently, she still appears to hold white Americans as the standard of beauty. She thinks blondes are prettier, and she feels "instantly jealous" when she sees a blonde person. She also equates being Filipina with certain physical characteristics such as "tan, dark hair, short, and flat face," and she commented that Filipinas tend to have flat noses, a negative feature. She recalls her mother and aunts pinching her nose as a child and commenting that it is important to not have a flat nose. In addition, her mother and aunts ingrained in her that Filipinas who appear *mestiza* (of mixed descent with European bloodlines), with fairer and lighter skin tones, are considered the prettiest. Her mother cautioned her to not play outside so that she would not become too dark. Despite these comments, Samantha then stated that she believes every woman is beautiful and that there should not be one standard of beauty. At the same time, she commented that she hates how she looks due to her nose flattening when she smiles, and she hates her "chubby" body shape and her face shape.

Be domesticated: Women in this study describe being taught feminine domesticity. They are trained to catch a man with their beauty, and that to keep him, they must be good with domestic chores. Within their own families, most women continue their domestic roles and are responsible for caring of the children, cooking, and cleaning. Maria noted the significance of these expectations as she referenced these expectations twice in the interview: "As for other expectations, marry a good husband, make sure he is Filipino, be a good mom, know how to cook… all the domestic kind of things." Later she repeated again: "There are definitely a good number of [Filipino] families that expect their daughters to marry a good husband, be the perfect wife, and know all the domestic chores, cook good food, cook good Filipino food." Emily shared a similar experience. She asserted

> You better learn how to cook, and you better clean without complaining… I have two new friends that are Filipino, and they cannot cook or boil water. I find that so weird. I'm like, "But you're Filipina. You should know. What did your mom do? Nothing?" I grew up with my mom telling me to be the homemaker but also have a career… the best of both worlds.

Daughters in second-class position: Enrile and Agbayani (2007) stated that Filipino women are viewed as inferior to Filipino men due to machismo and marianismo values. Marianismo is associated with the ideal of true femininity that women are supposed to live up to—i.e., being modest, morally upright, and sexually pure until marriage—and then being faithful and subordinate to their husbands. As such, parents from South and East Asian countries generally prefer sons to daughters. Raley and Bianchi (2006) pointed out that parents tend "to invest more resources in their sons, disproportionately abort female fetuses and sometimes resort to female infanticide." In this gendered context, daughters are expected to behave submissively to males in public, and are not always allowed the same privileges as their male siblings. In order to fulfill these centuries-old expectations, these Filipino American women are often perpetual second-class citizens in their own households. They are devalued and face marginalization in their home settings in contrast to male siblings.

As a female abiding by marianismo traditions, Sharon was expected to not have a boyfriend until she was at least eighteen years old. Further, she was required to help with household chores, behave respectfully, refrain from back talk, obey her parents, remain quiet, and be a doting daughter. She remembered how her father would wake her up early on the weekends so that she could clean the house, vacuum, do the laundry, wash the dishes, and put away objects before being allowed to engage in fun activities, while her brother played video games. Similarly, in Maria's family, her brother was treated differently than her and her half-sister. Even though Maria has a higher GPA than her brother, she was still expected to do more household chores than her brother. Further, her parents were less strict with him, affording him more freedom in terms of socializing and dating. When Maria expressed her anger about the unfairness to her mother, she replied "He's a guy." Likewise, Cathy noticed that her father continues to exhibit preferential treatment toward males during family parties. At those gatherings, she observed that her father offered beers only to the males but never offered Cathy a beer, despite Cathy was of legal drinking age. Her father's behavior made her question her worth. She thought "We're not good enough to have a beer? You don't think we can enjoy that kind of stuff?"

Contemporary female roles. In the past, many women had painfully given up their career dreams and higher education for feminine domesticity. But these contemporary Filipino American women were expected to obtain a higher education, perform well academically, and establish a successful career. For example, at thirty years old, Jessie's parents continue to push her to study and pass her nursing board exams. This is true of Maria's life as well. Like Jessie, her mother expected her to become a nurse and obtain high grades in school. Maria admitted that she has internalized this pressure to excel academically, characterizing herself as self-motivated and internally pressured to perform well in school.

Joanne, Kathleen, and Faith noted that in their experience, attending college is the minimum academic expectation for Filipino American women. Faith explained that attending college was never an uncertainty or a question but rather a reality that she was required to complete. Immigrant Filipino parents tend to drive their second-generation Filipino daughters to overachieve relative to the median level of education for most Americans. Such a high academic bar is set for these women. Indeed, this standard was met by many of the participants. The expectation of attainment of higher education that eventually led to gainful employment signifies a departure from traditional cultural values and is consistent with shifting expectations about Filipino daughters' roles in the family.

Further, most of the participants established professional careers. For example, their jobs include teacher, photographer and business owner, therapist, registered nurse, social worker, marketing manager, and financial aid counselor. Besides trying to aim high academically, it seems that Filipino American women are expected to be gainfully employed. Katie recalled that she saw these same values reflected in her own mother's behaviors. She characterizes her mother as an "independent woman" who stressed to Katie that America is full of opportunities for her to excel. Katie's mother reminded her:

> … to make something out of myself, whether it be a nurse or a doctor… Anyway, she was always hinting toward making a lot of money as an independent woman… As long as we have our own means of living and we're successful, and we love what we do, I think that's all she really wanted.

The expectation of academic success described as a stepping-stone to a better future with a good career and financial independence. Second-generation Filipino American women in this study expect to take on multiple roles. It is unclear whether some women would find this to be empowering, but Lynn perceived this as a burden. She stated

> When it comes to roles—even if you work—you're the housewife. You're the one always cleaning, doing everybody's laundry, and taking care of the kids… We're taken for granted for all the things that we do… It's just expected.

Like the expectation of having at least a college education, it seemed like the multiple roles held by Filipino American women stem from expectations of their family units and the Filipino community, and represent a minimum standard. Rather than recognizing how remarkable it is that these women function in their multiple roles, they are taken for granted and seen as ordinary, fulfilling only the minimum expectation. There is little fair exchange of household labor, even when these women bring money to the table.

Faith shared a similar experience regarding multiple roles: "We are strong because we can endure a lot… We take on the cooking and the cleaning… We bring the money at the same time, and stay on top of it to make sure our kids are not getting into things they're not supposed to be getting into… and then as a female, we have the added pressures to maintain our appearance… the dispersal of responsibility domestically does weigh heavily on the female more… almost always."

In the workplace and in other social settings, participants reported that they were also marginalized as females. Laura recalled that she was exposed to various insults and put-downs related to being female in professional settings. She recalled her male friends and male coworkers teasing her for being a "girl." During an internship at a social service agency, many male interns did not take her seriously and assumed she did not know much about videogames because she is female. Katie co-owns a photography business with her fiancé and feels devalued as a female in this joint venture, as only his name is included in the business name. Furthermore, when they have worked on various assignments, their clients assumed she is her fiancé's assistant. She also noticed that when she sends out e-mails with her signature, clients often reply by addressing their e-mails to her fiancé. Despite their website explaining that they work as a team, she said that clients often contacted her fiancé for inquiries and business needs. Working with her fiancé and the consequent reactions of clients have caused her to feel cast aside and dismissed as a woman. As a result, she felt the pressure to work harder and win more awards to obtain the same amount of recognition in the photography business as her male fiancé.

The Balancing Act: Gendered and Contemporary Roles

Through our interviews and analysis, we began to realize that second-generation American Filipinas, who are expected to assume both traditional and contemporary roles, suffer from several role issues. They suffer from role overload because on a day-to-day basis they shoulder multiple burdens of performing well at their outside jobs and be fully responsible at home. Hochschild (1989) used the term "second shift" to describe women who continue to be fully responsible at home after work outside the home. It is not uncommon for many of them to have serious problems involving physical, mental, and emotional exhaustion. Besides that, the demands of old and new values are in direct conflict with each other because the behaviors and attitudes expected in a work environment may be starkly different from the behaviors and attitudes at home. Thus these different sets of role requirements, very often at odd with each other, create role conflicts. In role overload, these women have to juggle and balance a multitude of responsibilities. In role conflict, they have to split themselves in two to do their jobs correctly.

It has been suggested that even though society is advancing, gender issues and bias are alive and well today (Risman 1998; Tichenor 2005; England 2010). Furthermore, machismo, an ideology that supports male dominance, was strongly encouraged during Spanish colonization has had a profound impact on gender attitudes toward Filipino women (Mananzan 1987). Historical, gender, cultural, and social structures continue to shape the identities of these women on individual, familial, and social levels. On one hand, they are expected to value family, be obedient to elders, maintain appearances, and complete domestic tasks. On the other hand, they are expected to excel academically, go to college, and develop successful careers. These expectations seem to coincide with the research of Enrile and Agbayani (2007), who noted that the gender roles of Filipino women are often conflicting, vacillating between egalitarian and patriarchal. It is often so ingrained in them that they do not recognize it. Instead, the participants eagerly took on more tasks at home and in the workplace simultaneously. With these multiple roles came multiple demands, but they seemed resigned to the fact that this is what they needed to do. They appeared to rationalize their assumption of multiple roles by stating that it was simply expected and quite normal to them to perform the gendered division of labor at home as well as to provide financial security for the family.

As daughters in Filipino households, they experienced being devalued because males are more valued than females. Additionally, Filipina Americans emphasized the value of female beauty. Some participants verbalized that it was preferred to have fair skin, an exotic *mestiza* look, elevated noses, and lighter eyes. Bulloch (2013) recognized that as a result of a long history of being colonized by the West, Filipinas tend to negatively compare their appearances against white Americans and believe that fairer skin is associated with higher socioeconomic status. While men are not held to the same standard, the gendered message Filipinas receive is to pursue beauty so that they can attract a husband. Expectations about appearance further reinforce an identity of inferiority among these women, as they are constantly bombarded with messages of not being beautiful enough.

Espiritu and Wolf (2001) found that Filipino Americans tend to have decreased self-esteem despite functioning seemingly well in terms of academics, work, and family. This seems to coincide with the experiences of this study's participants. The expectation to excel in all areas of life seems to be deeply ingrained in their identities as women. They seem to place value on themselves within the context of the success of their family relationships and are driven to achieve in order to sustain their families. Therefore, verbalizing protest or disagreement would reflect weakness as well as diminish a large part of their identities. As such, many of them may be suffering alone and in silence.

In summary, the female Filipino American participants in this study were born into and lived through a world of dissonant messages in terms of their cultural and gender identities. Many faced marginalization, criticism, messages of inferiority, and harsh expectations that have impacted their sense of self. Despite all of these experiences, they seem to have fulfilled their parents' dreams and expectations of living a life of opportunity in America. In some way, they have been able to navigate their incongruent and marginalizing experiences by adapting to both their dissonant internal and external worlds. None of these women may ever admit it, but they truly are quite exceptional.

Aiding Change: Strategies for Clinical Practice

Without exception, participants in this study experienced some form of marginalization due to their cultural backgrounds as a Filipina and a woman. Consequently, clinicians need to be aware of this phenomenon and take this into consideration when working with this population. Specifically, it may be helpful for assessment questions to focus on family immigration stories and cultural self-labels. Direct and specific questioning about how experiences associated with marginalization have impacted Filipino American clients' lives, self-concept, and behaviors may be helpful.

Another important area for clinical consideration is the multiple roles and expectations that many Filipino American women endure. Traditional models of being a woman are no longer the standard for this group, as many of them are required to function in many roles in the workplace, school, and family. The intersections of these multiple roles are likely to contribute to their general emotional and psychosocial functioning. Given that they have been socialized to view their multiple roles as normal rather than anything exceptional, they may not necessarily disclose in treatment that this is a source of stress for them. Clinicians need to be aware that these women may downplay or minimize their levels of distress. Additionally, Filipino American women may be unlikely to verbalize discomfort or feelings of being overwhelmed. Thus, it is important to screen for depression; symptoms may not be apparent, since they may present as rather high functioning. Strength-based models of therapy may be helpful to these high-achieving women who do not necessarily see their accomplishments for what they truly are. Looking at these issues through a gender lens and within the context of their relationships can help increase a clinician's understanding of their experiences.

Regarding interventions, clinicians should be mindful and careful in challenging dissonant thoughts and behaviors. Seemingly unhealthy fluctuations in self-perception and relationships, as well as inconsistent behaviors, may have an adaptive function for Filipino American women. In some cases, these dissonances allow them to be flexible, live in multiple worlds, and navigate the incongruent experiences that led to their internal dissonance in the first place. It may be helpful for clinicians to increase awareness of the conflicting messages derived from their experiences and contexts. Clinicians can also help these women reframe their seemingly incongruent behaviors and thoughts as adaptive and resilient, while also helping them recognize the unequal burdens they carry. It may be helpful for clinicians to normalize the need to have multiple identities, given their dissonant experiences and exposure to discrimination. Clinicians can work with these women to reinforce a positive narrative that supports their own constructions of gender identity within their cultural context. Therefore, taking a gender-equity perspective that considers how these women want to enact their multiple identities necessitates interventions targeted at empowering them to level their playing field.

References

Agbayani-Siewert, P. A., & Jones, L. (1997). Filipino American women, work, and family: An examination of factors affecting high labor force participation. *International Social Work, 40* (4), 407-423

Agbayani-Siewert, P. (2004). Assumptions of Asian American similarity: The case of Filipino and Chinese American students. *Social Work, 49*(1), 39-51.

Bulloch, H. M. (2013). Concerning constructions of self and other: auto-racism and imagining America in the christian Philippines. *Anthropological Forum, 23*(3), 221–241.

David, E. J. R., & Okazaki, S. (2006). The colonial mentality scale (CMS) for Filipino Americans: Scale construction and psychological implications. *Journal of Counseling Psychology, 53*, 241–252.

David, E. R. (2008). A colonial mentality model of depression for Filipino Americans. *Cultural Diversity and Ethnic Minority Psychology, 14*(2), 118-127. doi:10.1037/1099-9809.14.2.118

England, P. (2010). The gender revolution: Uneven and stalled. *Gender and Society, 24*(2), 149–166.

Enrile, A., & Agbayani, P. (2007). Differences in attitudes towards women among three groups of Filipinos: Filipinos in the Philippines, Filipino American immigrants, and U.S. born Filipino Americans. *Journal of Ethnic and Cultural Diversity In Social Work, 16*(1–2), 1–25.

Espiritu, Y.L. (1995). *Filipino American lives*. Philadelphia, PA: Temple University Press.

Espiritu, Y. L., & Wolf, D. (2001). The paradox of assimilation: Children of filipino immigrants in San Diego. In R. G. Rumbaut & A. Portes (Eds.), *Ethnicities: Children of Immigrants in America* (pp. 157–186). Berkeley and Los Angeles, CA: University of California Press.

Hochschild, A. (1989). *The Second Shift*. New York: Viking Penguin.

Heras, P. (2007). Psychotherapy with Filipinas. In D. M. Kawahara & O. M. Espin (Eds.), *Feminist Reflections on Growth and Transformation: Asian American Women in Therapy* (pp. 63–73). New York, NY: The Haworth Press Inc.

Mananzan, M. J, (1987) The Filipino Women: Before and After the Spanish Conquest of the Philippines. In M. J. Mananzan (Ed.), *Essays on Women* (pp. 6-35). Manila: The Institute of Women's Studies St. Scholastica's College

Nadal, K. L. (2011). *Filipino American Psychology: A Handbook of Theory, Research, and Clinical Practices*. Hoboken, NJ: Wiley.

Paul, A. M. (2015). Negotiating migration, performing gender. *Social Forces, 94*, 271–293.

Philpot, C., Brooks, G., Lusterman, D., & Nutt, R. (1997). *Bridging Separate Gender Worlds*. Washington, DC: American Psychological Association.

Raley, S. & Bianchi, S. (2006). Sons, Daughters, and Family Processes: Does Gender of Children Matter? *Annual Review of Sociology*, 32: 401-421

Risman, B. (1998). *Gender vertigo: American families in transition*. New Haven, CT: Yale University Press

Salam, R. A. (2005). *Am I South Asian? Personal, Organizational and Political Understandings of Second Generation South Asians' Ethnic Identity*. Conference Papers – American Sociological Association, (pp. 1–20).

Tichenor, V. (2005). Maintaining men's dominance: negotiating identity and power when she earns more. *Sex Roles, 53*(3/4), 191–205.

Tuason, T.G., Taylor, A. R., Rollings, L., Harris, T., & Martin, C. (2007). On both sides of the hyphen: Exploring the Filipino-American identity. *Journal of Counseling Psychology, 54*(4), 362-372.

Zhou, M., & Xiong, S. (2005). The multifaceted American experiences of the children of Asian immigrants: Lessons for segmented assimilation. *Ethnic and Racial Studies, 28*(6), 119-1152.

Chapter 8
Cultural Transmission to Cultural Transformation: The Case of Contemporary Chinese Americans in a Faith-Based Community

Peter C. Lim

"We are more American and feel that we should be able to make our own decisions… we should be respected. We are not kids anymore. *[But in our faith community]*…we are treated less than that or perceived as less than that, even though we have our own kids who are high schoolers." – the voice of a frustrated American born Chinese.

Every faith community has a cultural script. Understandably the Chinese church in America functions as a community of shared cultural beliefs and behaviors set apart from the American culture (Jeung 2005; Yang 1999). Historically its existence came about because language and cultural barriers prevented Chinese immigrants from assimilating into the dominant Anglo church. Coping with decades of intense immigration discrimination also encouraged the Chinese faith community cling to its ethnic identity (Alumkal 2003). Fear of cultural attrition due to assimilation intensifies the role of the Chinese church as the preserver and transmitter of its communal ethnic identity to the American-born generations. In choosing cultural transmission over cultural transformation, the Chinese church is socially wired to operate as an extended family system through its relational dynamics patterned after the Confucian hierarchy to support the cultural identity retention process. More than two decades after Helen Lee's seminal and provocative article (Lee 1996), "The Silent Exodus," generations of American-born Chinese continue to flee from their immigrant parents' church to escape this cultural entrapment.

Several ethnographic studies of Chinese Christians suggest that the ABC generation in the Chinese church often feels caught between two cultures (Jeung 2005; Cha et al. 2006; Yang 1999). These works focused on the role of the ethnic immigrant and Asian American churches and the challenges they faced in the identity construction of the American-born generation. What seems lacking is the understanding of the Chinese faith-based community as a system with family ties that can bind the healthy construction of the identity of the American-born generation. In this chapter, I

P.C. Lim (✉)
Ambassador NetWork, Brea, CA, USA
e-mail: peter-lim@bethel.edu

K.M.-T. Quek and S.-R.S. Fang (eds.), *Transition and Change in Collectivist Family Life*, AFTA SpringerBriefs in Family Therapy,
DOI 10.1007/978-3-319-50679-1_8

examine how the cultural tug-of-war between generations can be the space in which both generations become mutually enriching and empowering if they are willing to co-construct new ways of relating, learning, and leading. In family therapy, these hoped-for-solutions require members from each generation to collaborate and to avoid cut-offs (Friedman 1985).

I am a freelance church missional health consultant and strategist based in Southern California. I have invested many years studying and engaging American-born Chinese in their faith journey. Using participant observation as a methodology for this project, I participated actively in the activities of Chinese American churches for more than 15 years. Since the Chinese church is well known for assumptions and unspoken rules inherent in its Chinese way of doing things, I am interested in discovering the social construction of reality as experienced by American-born Chinese (ABCs) in the Chinese church. I am hopeful that family therapists will be informed about the relational issues within the Chinese faith community and be adept at translating this knowledge into cultural competent systemic therapy for Chinese Americans.

Method

This chapter is part of my doctoral dissertation that embraces a participatory observation approach to give voice to the disenfranchised ABC generation and to provide insights that may help to prevent their continued flight from the Christian faith community. Additionally, family therapists become clearer about assumptions that undergird Chinese family and their faith communities. These assumptions are translated into family therapy concepts (multigenerational transmission process, family projection process, togetherness, and separation) which unless recognized and corrected, produce generation after generation of similar familial patterns.

Thirty-five American-born Chinese whose ages range between 21 and 35 participated in one-on-one interviews. In total, 27 Chinese churches completed surveys consisted of general information to capture the demographic composition of the participant's church and the participant's cultural identity and motivations for staying in or leaving the Chinese faith community.

Findings

Based on the analyses from the interviews and church surveys, it is evident that there is more reality to the stereotypical contentious generational relationships in the Chinese church. On one hand, the competition for cultural allegiance to preserve their Chinese identity often exacts a big emotional toll as the American-born Chinese navigates between and betwixt their bicultural identities. On the other hand, generational tensions can be more benign and less conflictual when the strength of family ties is used to build and not to bind generational relationships.

Chinese Faith-Based Community as a Strong-Group Surrogate Family

Analysis concurs with Friedman's seminal work (1985), *Generation to Generation*, that illuminates how relational dynamics in this type of faith community mirror the emotional processes of the families that make up the church itself. From an observation of the groups within the Chinese churches in this study, the Chinese faith community is not only made up of families and focused on families, it is run like a big, extended family with multiple generations under one roof. This parallels the traditional definition of a Chinese family that includes a wide network of kinship (Guo 1995). In traditional Chinese families, the children are not raised solely by their parents, but are cared for by a wide range of related adults, such as grandparents, uncles, aunts, cousins, and even wet nurses. Likewise, as a family system, the Chinese faith community is a complex organization with multigenerational and multicultural components.

Most interviewees report they find the hierarchical structure within the faith community stifling. Tony, an ABC from a Chinese Church in CA, remarked "When we fail to follow the structure, not only have I failed, but I am a failure." Most remark that they saddled with the moral obligations of compliance because of their generational status in the family system of a Chinese church. This parent–child dynamic, coupled with the "interesting integration of Confucianism and Christianity," helps the church "become an institutional base for passing on transformed Confucian values to younger generations" (Yang 1999, p. 51). This faith community acts as a living cultural repository for the American-born generation. The cultural conformity focuses on external behavior change by enforcing cultural rules and norms, spoken and unspoken.

Preserving Chinese Cultural Tradition

Most interviewees express frustration as they perceive the immigrant generation as stubbornly clinging to traditions of their country of origin, traditions that they themselves are not naturally drawn to inherit or preserve. Besides operating the church community like an extended family, many interviewees also share about cultural preservation from the Confucian and Christian teachings. For instance, in church they learn about the fifth of the Ten Commandments that provides a nuance that relates honoring parents as an act of filial piety. The word *honor* is translated as "孝 敬"(*xiao jing*) instead of simply as "尊敬" (*zun jing*). The latter means "respect" and that is how most of the American-born generation will understand the word "honor." But the Chinese translation of Deuteronomy 5:16 demands honoring one's parents as an act of filial piety since the word "孝" (*xiao*) means being filial. In fact, the logogram of the Chinese character for filial piety, 孝(xiào), shows the younger/older dichotomy with the character of an old man over a younger person. This indicates how the Chinese virtue of filial piety is endorsed through the Bible. This virtue depicts a relational dynamic that is clearly influenced by the age or rank of the relational hierarchy, requiring the obeisance and respect of the younger person toward the older. Conflict arises as both generations read the fifth commandment from different cultural and generational lenses (Ge 1998).

There are tensions between the immigrant and the American-born Chinese when one generation uses religious participation and the use of Christian teachings to maintain their ethnic culture and social networks while the other generation finds it burdensome to continue to uphold such traditions. The family system in the Chinese church tends to reinforce the cultural expectations of the social obligations of children toward parent, deference to opinions and wishes of parents over the children's desires. They do so by reconstructing the Confucian family values and traditions through modifying the moral vocabulary from one of filial pieties to religious discipleship. Consistent with findings in this study, Chen (2006) observed that "Taiwanese parents used evangelical Christianity to reproduce some traditional Taiwanese values by morally reframing these as acts of Christian discipleship rather than using the Confucian vocabulary of family duty" (p. 575). Obedience to God now provides the moral authority that parents have over their children. Christian discipleship in the Chinese church frames the familial codes of parent–child relationship as one of personal choices—the choice one has in obeying God. Chris' incendiary comment about the role of culture in his Chinese church illustrates this frustration:

> It is amazing that when you take the Chinese culture and combine it with the mid-west conservative evangelical thought, you get a wonderful synergism. [I] am already feeling insecure of my performance because of my parents who are pushing me to do better in school … with the American dream that I am pursuing, and my parents wanting to see me do better than they do. I have the pressure to be good Chinese children in our Chinese sub-culture in the US… and that I don't want to do anything that will shame the family or create disharmony. … You put those things together you have the capacity to manipulate people to love God and to follow the church.

Under such cultural script, the Chinese faith community duplicates the dominant relationship of a parent–child dyad with the Confucian dictum that "parents are always right" (Hsu 1981, p. 79). In this context, the English congregation comprising the American-born Chinese, many of whom are children of members in the Chinese congregation, assumes the role of the child while the Chinese congregation assumes the role of parental leadership and authority. While the filial obligation of this parent–child dyad helps in the transmission of culture, the same relational dynamic is often stifling for the identity development of the American-born generation. Here is what Joshua has to say about his Chinese church in Chicago:

> We are more American and feel that we should be able to make our own decisions… we should be respected. We are not kids anymore. *In fact, we are not your kids!* We are not related to you! … [*But under the cultural script constructed*] …as a whole the English congregation comprising all the American born Chinese is related to the Chinese congregation. We are being perceived as their kids. Sometimes you are just too old to feel like that…to be someone's kids. If you fight your way through and get connected with people, then you are fine. If you don't, there is a disconnect with the other aspects of your life. I am well respected and honored at work but to be in the English Congregation where all the American born Chinese come together, we are treated less than that or perceived as less than that even though we have our own kids who are high schoolers.

Given this parent–child relational dynamic between the Chinese and English congregations, the authoritarian and directive Chinese parenting style presents a real challenge. Any perceived problem behavior from the American-born generation is often thought to be due to a lack of discipline of the child. When the younger generation tries to show autonomy in making decisions, acting like autonomous Americans, it is often perceived as an attack on the immigrant generation. The latter would view such attacks as cultural deviations of the younger generation and dislike of their Chinese identity, while the former would think of it as their coming of age process in independent decision-making. Self-reliance and autonomy are the American hallmarks of identity formation (Hofstede 2001). Most participants remark that the pressures of a strong-group culture just strike their generation as restrictive, if not somewhat oppressive. And because of the deeply embedded Confucian propriety of "saving face" to maintain respect for the older immigrant generation, they often feel disempowered in the Chinese church community, lacking a voice to make their own decision (Ge 1998). They are expected to "keep quiet" or show deference to the older generation whenever there are differences. As a result, participants from this study state that they are emotionally drained and think that they do not have a voice. They are unsure about their identity formation within the Chinese faith community.

In fact, the struggle for autonomy to develop their identity, especially when it involves cultural deviations, is sometimes identified as a problem that necessitates corrective and disciplinary actions. Typical behavior correction includes shame-based and duty-bound compliance and submission to those in authority (i.e., the immigrant generation) to maintain harmony and achieve the greater good for the community. On other occasions, the American-born generation is extolled to practice the virtue of "eating bitterness," (吃苦, chī kǔ), a Chinese virtue of enduring hardship for the sake of character formation. This strategy is often used to extract loyalty from the second-generation Chinese when they resist complying with parental or the immigrant generation's demands. This relational dynamic is disempowering for the American-born Chinese. It isolates them as the problem to be solved while leaving the unhealthy communal/family system that maintains the tension between the generations intact.

Chinese Identity in This Surrogate Family

The issue of personal identity is at the very heart of the generational tensions in the Chinese church community. Performing as a surrogate family, the Chinese faith community in the United States plays a powerful role in the retention and transmission of their ethnic identity in their second-generation members while helping the immigrant generation assimilate to life in the United States. For this reason, the findings suggest that many Chinese families come to the Chinese Christian communities of faith to enable their children to have an exposure to Chinese culture and be connected with their Chinese American peers in the church (Alumkal 2003). Chinese Christian parents often turn to these faith communities to make sure their kids are "on the right track." The expectations of the immigrant parents are often centered on the identity formation of their children. They expect the faith community to help develop good *Chinese* Christians out of their children, with the unspoken emphasis on being good Chinese. Often the interviewees report that the immigrant generation tends to address such hopes in the language of spiritual identity formation. Here is how Daniel, a second-generation Youth Pastor Intern in a Chinese church, views his Chinese church as shaping the ABC generation to be good Chinese more than being good Christians:

> The pressure on the younger generation to be good Chinese Christians whose performance in schools and vocational track in college … heavy expectations on youth, not just for academic performance that their lives will look a certain way. I felt a tension between parents and youths … sometimes what their parents want is not necessarily what their youths want … what these Chinese parents want is for the youth group to serve as a surrogate parent for some of these kids to help them to behave well and to keep them out of trouble…make sure they are encouraged to do well in school … at times *I felt that tension because my priority is for discipleship and spiritual formation but they are interested in that as a secondary goal; their primary goal would be "I want my kids to respect me, do well in school, be obedient."* Sometimes I tell the parents that I am not your kids' parents (emphasis mine).

Preserving the Chinese ethnic identity is paramount to the immigrant generation. The Chinese ethnic self is understood in one's connectedness to a network of familial and social relationships. This self-definition contrasts with the mainstream American individualistic self in that the self in the dominant American society is individuated, self-contained, and separate, being defined by clear boundaries from others (Hofstede 2005). The Chinese ethnic self is more of an interdependent, relational self (Kagititcibasi 2007). A Chinese individual typically subordinates personal interests to group interests. To discover and develop the self-identity, one needs to inquire into the interconnected nature of relationships and to uncover some of the principles embedded in those relationships. Ge (1996) writes "self in the Confucian sense is defined by a person's surrounding relations, which often are derived from kinship networks and supported by cultural values such as filial piety, loyalty, dignity, and integrity (p. 83)" For example, Chinese often stress social interactions and describe themselves in terms of social roles. They often feel the need to uphold culturally endorsed aspects of the self to gain positive appraisal by others.

The relational tension heightens between the immigrant and the second generations due to one generation who wants to preserve the Chinese ethnic identity that stresses the importance of the collective over the individual, while the American-born generation wants to embrace the American cultural paradigm of individualism. Instead of pitting autonomy against relatedness, it is better to recognize that autonomy and relatedness are both basic human needs (Knudson-Martin 1994). Any family context that satisfies and reinforces these two needs would be a stronger family with individual members who develop strong individual identity while remaining connected to the community. Given the construal of the Chinese self, an individual's identity involves multiple layers of relations with others, with sensitivity to the hierarchical positions of these relationships. This paradigm corresponds with Kagitcibasi (2007)'s concept of the autonomous-related self, in which she questions the claim that one has to separate in order to develop autonomy. Similarly, the biblical concept of self also endorses this idea of the development of self-identity in relation to and in the context of a community. However, for the Chinese faith community, balancing between togetherness and separation with the goal of achieving an autonomous-related self is still a work in progress.

The importance of group interest and kinship connectedness in defining "self" in the Chinese culture presents unique challenges. Confucian principles provide the basis for organizational bureaucracy that calls for loyalty through submission and conformity to group goals. The individuals are perceived as part of a network of social relations, in which they find their own identities with reference to the group. Individuals exist for the benefit of the group, and adopt group goals and opinions. According to Triandis (1989), the self is considered to have three distinct dimensions: private (what I think of myself), public (what other people think of me), and collective (what specific groups of people think of me). The Chinese conception of "big me" (大我, dà wǒ, the group) and "little me" (小我, xiǎo wǒ, the individual) illustrates the subordination of the individual identity to the collective identity. It is expected of the individual, the "little me" to make sacrifices to complete the big me—牺牲小我, 成全大我 (xīshēng xiǎo wǒ, chéngquán dà wǒ). Successful ethnic self-identity is measured by one's ability and willingness to maintain interdependence between the individual and the group, rather than by a process of separation and individuation as conceptualized in Western psychological theories.

The mainstream American concept of individualism is often frowned upon because it appears to the immigrant generation as selfishness or self-centeredness—an unnatural attempt to isolate the self from the group and to prioritize personal interests over group interests. As a result, the Chinese church community typically places stronger emphasis in maintaining togetherness and harmony. These concepts tend to rank higher than autonomy and self-actualization needs of the individuals. De-emphasizing the individual interest and the reinforcement for group harmony is supported by the Chinese cultural traits of being reserved, restrained, and respectful (in a formal way); but being restricted in expressions of personal feelings and opinions is the disempowerment of the ABC generation. In fostering a successful relationship between the "big me" and the "little me," the Chinese culture teaches individuals to be concerned about how others will react or what others think so that they can maintain face. If one does not fulfill expectations of the group on self, then one loses face and therefore experiences shame and loses self-confidence. This is both the contributing factor and outcome of the low differentiation in the relational dynamics between generations in the Chinese faith community.

Implications

When cultural transmission is enabled by the embedded Chinese family systemic values and dynamics in the faith community, it creates a stuckness between the generations. Such relational dynamics is stifling to the American-born Chinese who wants greater autonomy and self-expression. This stuckness makes the search for a balance between generational relations in a bicultural Chinese church like a quixotic quest. Whereas it is necessary for any individual to discover one's identity in relationship within a community, the group-centeredness of the Chinese faith community presents challenges for American-born Chinese. Often the individual's identity is defined by the group goals and community-defined expectations. Success or failure in life is measured by how well the individuals do in attaining these group goals and community-defined expectations.

Neither social orientation of individualism nor collectivism is intrinsically good or bad. The strong-group orientation of the Chinese faith community can be stifling to the individuation process of the American-born generation. Locating the individual in a relational system according to their rank, role and responsibility pressures the American-born Chinese to conform culturally to the immigrant generation. The Chinese faith community then teeters constantly on the edge of generational tensions, and often maintains social harmony by enforcing the authoritarian and paternalistic control of the immigrant generation. Under such circumstances, the generational tension creates the kind of emotional anxiety that ultimately hampers healthy identity development among the American-born generation. Unfortunately, many choose to leave such communities to find breathing room for their development, but only to find themselves needing years of recovery because they have only left physically and not emotionally.

Intervention requires a larger systemic change, i.e., developing a healthy family system in the Chinese church that recognizes the need for balance between separateness and togetherness. As Augsburger (1986) emphasized, the individual self can only be defined and differentiated in the context of a relationship to a group. Neither the Chinese faith community's group-centeredness nor the American-born Chinese's search for individuality has to be sacrificed in the process of defining self. Augsburger (1986) summed up this balance well:

> The individual-in-community is the primary unit of humanness. …Humanness is not individually defined, nor is it a description of all the uniqueness, variation, or possibilities within community. … Persons, as individuals in their respective communities, are irreducibly valuable, of unalterable worth, and are to be prized as ends in themselves. Thus neither the community nor the individual is to be valued above the other. Both find maturity in the balanced prizing and integration with each other (p. 108).

The irony of striving harder to be a family to provide a safe space to transmit culture is that it inadvertently builds emotional barriers and gridlocks that causes the ABCs to resist being conformed to that culture. Instead, the Chinese faith community can provide a safe space that balances togetherness and separation in such a way that the individuals among the American-born generation feel supported by the community. Stripping the quintessential strong-group culture off its "group-before-self" trademark will create emotional space for greater interdependence in the community. That in turn supports the individuals among the ABCs to discover and develop their personal identity in the context of relationship with significant others. When this happens, there is greater likelihood for members of the younger generation to blend and integrate the opposing influences stemming from the liminality of their bicultural identity into a more cohesive identity. In many social situations, second-generation Chinese Americans will be defined by their "Chinese-ness," even in this era of multiculturalism. This identity is used as a tool to define themselves in relation to others. Sometimes they are compelled to demonstrate their Chinese cultural competence and authenticity even while they are asserting their "American-ness." If the challenges of transmitting the cultural heritage to the ABCs can be understood as bringing what is best about the past to create what is promising for the future, the focus will be shifted from cultural transmission to cultural transformation. This type of paradigm shift is the second-order change in systemic therapy where change has happened in the rules that govern the internal structure.

In clinical practice, therapists who work with the Chinese immigrant and American-born generations need to connect with and validate them simultaneously. Both individuals in differing generations have their own version of reality, which causes a cultural collision. It will also be helpful to note that both generations share the similar goal to reclaim community (ChenFeng et al. 2015). Therapists can help them define and reclaim a new type of community that appropriated elements of Chinese cultural traditions, various expressions of mainstream American culture and biblical teachings. As both generations work on their shared future, they should be encouraged to imagine creative ways in which they would like to realize their preferred future. Both generations must understand that cultural differences can provide richness and choice, and they are not "right" or "wrong" choices, nor are they "good" or "bad" choices. Instead, they can creatively think of integrating cultural traditions to create new "rituals" for both generations to share in the church, embracing and celebrating the legacy of both cultures. At the same time, they can maintain a flexibility to accommodate different interests and needs of each sub-group by retaining appropriate traditional rituals where possible. It is necessary to be flexible and tolerant to find the best way of satisfying as many of the needs of both generations as possible, whether separately or together. They should concentrate on important situations only, the ones that can create meaning to both generations in the Chinese faith community.

References

Alumkal, A. (2003). *Asian American Evangelical churches: Race, ethnicity, an assimilation in the second generation*. New York: LFB Scholarly Publishing LLC.

Augsburger, D. (1986). *Pastoral counseling across cultures*. Philadelphia, PA: The Westminster Press.

Cha, P., Kang, S., & Lee, H. (2006). *Growing Healthy Asian American Churches*. Downers Grove, IL: Intervarsity Press.

Chen, C. (2006). From filial piety to religious piety: Evangelical christianity reconstructing Taiwanese immigrant families in the United States. *The International Migration Review, 40*(3), 573–602. doi:10.1111/j.1747-7379.2006.00032.x.

ChenFeng, J., Knudson-Martin, C., & Nelson, T. (2015). Intergenerational tension, connectedness and separateness in the lived experience of first and second generation Chinese American Christians. *Contemporary Family Therapy*. doi:10.1007/s10591-015-9335-9.

Friedman, E. (1985). *Generation to Generation*. New York, NY: The Guilford Press.

Ge, G. (1996). Self and other: A Chinese perspective on interpersonal relationships. In W. Gudykunst, S. Ting-Toomey, & T. Nishida (Eds.), *Communication in Personal Relationships across Cultures* (pp. 81–101). Thousand Oaks, CA: SAGE Publications.

Ge, G. (1998). An analysis of the effects of face and concern for "other" in Chinese communication. *International Journal of Intercultural Relations, 22*, 467–482.

Guo, Z. (1995). Chinese Confucian culture and the medical ethical tradition. *Journal of Medical Ethics, 21*, 239–246.

Hofstede, G. (2001). *Culture's consequences*. Newbury Park, CA: Sage.

Hofstede, G. (2005). *Culture's consequences*. Newbury Park, CA: Sage.

Hsu, F. L. K. (1981). *Americans and Chinese*. Honolulu, HI: University of Hawaii Press.

Jeung, R. (2005). *Faithful generations: Race and new Asian American churches*. London: Rutgers University Press.

Kagititcibasi, C. (2007). *Family, Self, and Human Development across Cultures*. Mahwah, NJ: Lawrence Erlbaum Associates.

Knudson-Martin, C. (1994). The female voice: Applications to Bowen's family systems theory. *Journal of Marital and Family Therapy, 20*(1), 35–46.

Lee, H. (1996). Silent exodus: Can the East Asian church in America reverse the flight of its next generation? *Christianity Today, 40*, 9.

Triandis, H. (1989). The self and social behavior in differing cultural contexts. *Psychological Review, 96*(3), 506–520.

Yang, F. (1999). *Chinese Christians in America*. Philadelphia, PA: The Pennsylvania State University Press.

Chapter 9
Bicultural Identity as a Protective Factor Among Southeast Asian American Youth Who Have Witnessed Domestic Violence

Skultip (Jill) Sirikantraporn

Domestic Violence and Southeast Asian American Youth

Children and youth who are exposed to domestic violence (DV) often experience mental, emotional, and social harms that can affect their developmental growth. Exposure to DV may occur in the form of seeing the actual incidents of abuse between the caregivers; hearing threats or fighting noises; observing the aftermath of the violence (e.g., bruises, blood, broken objects); and being aware of the tension and fear at home. Many youth experience guilt and engage in self-blame for the abuse at home, for not being able to protect the abused caregiver, and/or for being angry at one or both caregivers (National Crime Victimization Survey 2008). Exposure to DV may then result in hopelessness, helplessness, depression, anxiety, somatic symptoms (e.g., headaches, stomachaches, bedwetting), and other trauma-related symptoms (Rossman 2001). These consequences are exacerbated in youth due to their age-limited cognitive and developmental capacity to make sense of the violence at home.

Many Southeast Asian American (SEAA) youths witness DV in their families. Approximately 40–60% of Asian women in the United States have reported experiencing physical and sexual violence at the hands of their intimate partners (Yoshihama and Dabby 2015). In addition, over 45% of Southeast Asian Americans reported knowing someone during their lifetime who has lived in a domestic violence situation (Yoshihama and Dabby 2015). The actual prevalence of violence among SEAA families is difficult to know. Research suggests that the known rates may likely be lower than reality, as Asian victims in the United States are less likely to report intimate partner violence (National Asian Women's Health Organization 2002). Due to cultural, linguistic, and social barriers, many SEAA victims are unable

S. (Jill) Sirikantraporn (✉)
California School of Professional Psychology, Alliant International University, San Diego, CA, USA
e-mail: ssirikantraporn@alliant.edu

K.M.-T. Quek and S.-R.S. Fang (eds.), *Transition and Change in Collectivist Family Life*, AFTA SpringerBriefs in Family Therapy,
DOI 10.1007/978-3-319-50679-1_9

to acknowledge and speak out about DV. Many Asian values emphasize familial harmony over an individual's needs and encourage "saving face" by not sharing negative family matters with others in order to preserve family pride (Kramer et al. 2002). In addition, many SEAA victims may not want to risk being alienated from their ethnic community by speaking out about DV, which is often seen as a "Western" problem that does not exist within their ethnic culture (Southeast Asia Resource Action Center [SARAC] 2003). A mistrust of United States authorities and fear of deportation may also discourage many victims from reporting. Moreover, many SEAA families lack awareness and knowledge about accessing mental health services. These factors create confusion and additional pressure to keep DV a family secret, which in turn puts children who witness the violence at greater risk. Considering these factors, I believe that more understanding and targeted research should be done to shed more light on the impact of DV on SEAA youth.

Domestic Violence and Resilience Among Youth

Domestic violence is an extreme risk for youth that weakens their resilience. Resilience is defined as reduced vulnerability to environmental risks, and the ability to overcome a stress or adversity, with relatively good outcomes despite risk experiences (Rutter 1987). Many children who witness DV are at risk of being abused and neglected themselves. In addition, those who witness DV may internalize violence as a way to resolve conflicts, which further diminishes their ability to learn healthy ways to form relationships outside of their families (Rossman 2001). Youth resilience literature concurs that one of the most essential protective factors for youth against psychopathology is the presence of caring and nurturing caregivers and family relationships (Rutter 1987). This factor plays a crucial role in boosting youths' ability to develop positively and bounce back successfully from life stressors. Violence between their caregivers, however, means that this very important protective factor may be disrupted and compromised, which puts youth at great risk of developing maladjustment problems. This phenomenon has already been observed among Southeast Asian youth in one study, which found that youth who reported that their parents "talked nicely and did not yell" adjusted significantly better academically than those who did not (Xiong et al. 2005). This led me to hypothesize that SEAA youth who have witnessed DV would be less resilient than youth who have not.

Acculturation Among SEAA Youth and Resilience

Acculturation continues to be the central focus when researchers discuss the health and well-being of immigrants. I therefore focused my research on this concept as it pertains to SEAA youth. Southeast Asian immigrants, including Vietnamese,

Cambodian, Laotian, and other ethnic groups residing in these countries such as Hmong, Mien and Cham, account for one of the most rapidly growing immigrant groups in the United States (SARAC 2003). Asian immigrants are often grouped together as one homogenous cultural group in research studies, which undermines a clear understanding of the unique needs and histories of Asian subgroups. For SEAA immigrants, the experience of immigration is often fraught with trauma before, during and after immigration. For instance, following the Khmer Rouge atrocity and the Vietnam War, Southeast Asian immigrants and their children fled their homes and started to immigrate to the United States since the late 1970s. Several sociocultural factors, such as exposure to war-related trauma in their home countries, a loss of socioeconomic status, and acculturative stress upon immigration to the United States may contribute to high familial and marital discord, which may in turn lead to or exacerbate domestic violence (Chan 2004).

Many Southeast Asian refugees immigrated with their young children. Southeast Asian youth who are either American born or immigrated with their parents at a very young age experience an immigration and acculturative process that is unique and often different from that of their parents (Serafica 1997). Children are often found to acculturate to the host culture (the United States in this case) faster than their parents due to early exposure to English training and socialization into American values. These differences may lead to acculturation gaps among SEAA families that can be a source of conflict (Sue and Sue 2008), which further complicates how SEAA youth cope with DV.

Acculturation literature suggests that it is not the process of acculturation itself that is positive or negative for immigrant youths' adjustment; instead, the levels of acculturation play a crucial role (Dinh et al. 2008; Xiong et al. 2005). As youth attempt to establish their own cultural identities that are influenced by both the host culture and their parents' native cultures, they often experience pressure to resolve differences between these two sets of culture. This process has implications for youths' adjustment and well-being. Berry's theory of acculturation (Berry 2001) suggests that there are four levels of acculturation: integrative (biculturalism), assimilation (highly identified with the host culture), separation (highly identified with the native culture), and marginalization (identified with neither cultures).

Of the four-acculturation levels, biculturalism has been found to be associated with positive adjustment to the new culture (Berry 2001). Several studies in Asian populations have also found bicultural identity to be a positive factor in relation to adolescents' health and well-being (Nguyen and Benet-Martínez 2007; Xiong et al. 2005). One positive characteristic of biculturalism can be seen as the ability to flexibly negotiate the demands of the social context that arise from two cultures without compromising one's sense of cultural identity (Vargas-Reighley 2005). In the face of adversity, bicultural competence affords youth flexible problem-solving and coping capabilities (Vargas-Reighley 2005). The ability to comfortably communicate in both languages facilitates youths' socialization, decreases social isolation, and increases success in help-seeking behavior (Dinh et al. 2008; Vargas-Reighley 2005). The increased social competence and communication ability in both cultural settings found in bicultural youth may reduce the impact of isolation, confusion, and threats to safety for those living in households with DV. This led me to hypothesize that among SEAA youth who have witnessed DV, those who identified themselves as bicultural would show the highest level of resilience, compared with those who identified themselves as highly Asian or highly Americanized.

Method

In order to test my hypotheses, I conducted a cross-sectional quantitative study, exploring the relationship between three main variables: Southeast Asian American youths' experiences witnessing domestic violence, their level of acculturation, and their level of resilience.

I recruited participants from two community-based organizations (located in the Northwest and Northeast United States) that provide youth development programs for Southeast Asian American youth. These organizations provide comprehensive social services (such as mental health counseling, case management, English and citizenship classes, youth social skills groups, and youth violence prevention programs) to Asian American youth. The youth were recruited from local schools and voluntarily signed up to be part of the youth programs. All participants were from the weekly youth groups that met between December 2007 and February 2008. A total of 83 youth completed the study materials. The participating youth (whose ages ranged from 13 to 18) were informed of the purpose of the study, including the voluntary basis of participation, confidentiality issues, compensation for the study, and mental health service referrals when needed. Youths' assent and parental consent for all participating youth were obtained. All but one participant (N = 82) had at least one parent who had emigrated from a Southeast Asian country (Cambodia, Laos, Myanmar or Vietnam) and were included in the analysis.

All participants completed the following measures:

Demographic form: This page included general background information regarding school, grade, gender, age, specific ethnicity (how they identified themselves ethnically), length of residence in the United States, and the length of their participation in the youth program.

The 5-item witnessing domestic violence questionnaire: The questionnaire was based on the definition of DV set forth by the National Crime Victimization Survey (2008). Youth who answered "yes" to at least one of the questions were grouped as "having witnessed DV" and youth who answered "no" to all the questions were grouped as "not having witnessed DV." This study only examined the reported experiences of those who have and have not witnessed DV. The severity of the DV was not explored in this study. The questions were as follows:

- Have you ever heard one of your caregivers put down the other caregiver in front of others?

- Have you ever heard one of your caregivers call the other caregiver names when angry?
- Have you ever seen one of your caregivers push, kick, punch, slap, hit or hurt the other caregiver?
- Have you ever heard one of your caregivers threaten to hurt the other caregiver or to hurt him/herself?
- Have you ever had the impression that one of your caregivers does not feel safe at home because of potential violence from the other caregiver?

Youth Risk and Resilience Inventory (YRRI): The YRRI was used to measure youth participants' resilience levels. The YRRI was designed to screen for the presence of risk and resilience factors to identify signs of emotional stress and personal assets to assess their impact on the individual. For the purpose of this study, I administered the 18-item Resilience Factors. The YRRI has been used in youth substance abuse programs, youth correctional facilities, and domestic and family violence programs and shelters (Brady 2007). The scores were categorized into five levels of resilience based on the cutoff raw scores: 1 = very low, 2 = low, 3 = average, 4 = high, and 5 = very high.

Suinn-Lew Asian Self-identity Acculturation Scale (SL-ASIA): This measurement of acculturation among Asian Americans was adapted from a similar scale used to measure acculturation among Hispanics, called The Acculturation Rating Scale for Mexican Americans (Suinn 2001). The 21-item SL-ASIA is a standardized Likert-scale measurement that has been tested for validity and reliability for measuring acculturation and self-identification in relation to several aspects of Asian culture, such as language, music–movie preference, food consumption, and ethnic self-identification (Suinn 2001). Each question is measured on a 5-point scale, where choice 1 is indicative of high Asian identity (Asian-identified) and choice 5 is indicative of high Western identity (Western-identified). A score of 3 is classified as bicultural. The scale was initially found to have a 0.88 alpha coefficient, and subsequent studies have reported similar alpha coefficients from 0.86 to 0.88 (Chung et al. 2000).

Results

A total of 82 youth participated in the study, their ages ranging from 13 to 18 years old with the mean age of 16.25. The ethnic groups represented by the youth participants were as follows: Cambodian (21.9%), Vietnamese (18.3%), Mien (14.6%), Laotian (12.2%), and other Southeast Asian ethnic groups and/or combinations of ethnic groups (33%). Of 82 youth, 59 youth (71.95%) reported having witnessed at least one type of DV.

Domestic Violence and Resilience

The study findings supported the first hypothesis. The t-test analysis was used to find the mean difference in the level of resilience between the youth who had witnessed domestic violence (n = 59) and those who had not (n = 23). Youth who had witnessed domestic violence scored significantly lower on the resilience level (M = 3.40, SD = 0.94) than those who had not (M = 3.86, SD = 0.57), t = 2.30, p = 0.05.

Acculturation and Resilience

The results also supported the second hypothesis, which predicted a curvilinear relationship between the levels of acculturation and resilience among youth who had witnessed domestic violence (n = 59). The author used the scatter plot graph option in Microsoft Excel StatPlus and curve estimation within the regression analysis in SPSS to analyze the relationship. A curvilinear relationship between the level of acculturation and resilience was observed. The quadratic analysis yielded a significant increase in prediction, R = 0.259, $p = 0.001$. The results indicated that the youth who had witnessed domestic violence and who were bicultural scored highest on the resilience level, compared with those who were highly Asian or highly Westernized.

Discussion

I examined two relationships in this study: the impact of DV exposure and Southeast Asian youths' levels of resilience, and the levels of acculturation and resilience between those who had and those who had not witnessed DV. The results of this study showed that SEAA youth who reported witnessing DV scored lower on their resilience scale, which supported my first hypothesis. These findings confirmed what is known in the literature—that DV is a risk factor that diminishes youths' resilience. Disrupted family cohesion resulting from DV may indicate the absence of an important protective factor for youth development, that of a nurturing and caring familial environment. This may expose youth to multiple additional risks, including being the direct victim of abuse and neglect, interrupted healthy communication and socialization, and disrupted academic support at home.

While negative consequences of DV on youth have been elucidated, many youth who witness DV also exhibit resilience or the ability to bounce back from the distress (Martinez-Torteya et al. 2009). Among SEAA youth, the role of acculturation as a protective factor had not yet been explored. I hypothesized that among those who had witnessed DV, youth who self-identify as bicultural (the integrated level of acculturation) would score higher on resilience. This hypothesis was also supported. The results indicated that bicultural youth were the most resilient despite having witnessed domestic violence. The level of resilience was lower among youth who were self-rated as highly Asian or highly Westernized. This finding was consistent with those of several studies supporting the theory that biculturalism is related to positive adaptation despite life stress among immigrant youth (Castro et al. 2007; Xiong et al. 2005). In the presence of domestic violence, which often disrupts nurturing bonds and communication between caregivers as well as between youth and their caregivers, youths' ability to reach out and form relationships in outside social settings becomes extremely essential. Bicultural youth may possess cultural flexibility, cultural identity cohesion and linguistic abilities that allow them to confidently and competently communicate with both the host culture and their parents' native cultures. This in turn may alleviate isolation and increase their ability to cope with stress at home.

There were some limitations in this study. First, the study used convenience sampling by recruiting youth from the youth programs organized by community-based organizations. This limits the findings' generalizability in relation to other Southeast Asian youth populations due to a possible self-selection bias. Second, the small sample presents another generalizability limitation, and the findings should be considered preliminary. Lastly, the severity of DV (e.g., how many forms of DV did the youth witness?) was not examined because the study was designed to compare youth who had and youth who had not witnessed DV. Future research should examine the effects of the severity of DV that youth witness on their resilience.

Clinical Implications

Based on my study's findings and relevant literature, I would like to offer a few suggestions for mental health professionals when working with SEAA youth and families. First, the large percentage of youth who reported having witnessed domestic violence highlights the need for a domestic violence screening tool for Southeast Asian populations and culturally relevant psychoeducation on domestic violence. The educational materials and the screening tool should be available in different Southeast Asian languages, such as Khmer, Vietnamese and Lao, for youth and their parents who may be more comfortable with their native languages. Screening should also be incorporated into regular examinations in educational and healthcare settings to capture youth and parents who otherwise would not volunteer their DV experiences.

Second, mental health professionals should take possible cultural differences into account to better serve the SEAA population. For instance, different views of what constitutes domestic violence may hinder communication between a client and mental health clinician. For example, physical and emotional violence may be tolerated and/or accepted in some SEAA families and may not be easily detected without the appropriate level of rapport with clinicians and culturally respectful psychoeducation about DV. Acculturation also plays an important role. Information from this study helps to guide mental health professionals and youth programs in proactively assessing youths' acculturation level from the youths' own perspectives and acknowledging the strengths and challenges associated with those varying degrees of acculturation. A bicultural level of acculturation has been shown to be a protective factor for an ethnic minority population, and therefore bicultural self-efficacy training is recommended to alleviate these problems. Bicultural skills and competence training programs are recommend, as they may serve to strengthen both a youth's Southeast Asian and Asian American identities, which may be a protective factor to further prevent bicultural stress or to assuage the impact of it.

Third, it has been suggested that the influence of the acculturative process among minority youth may be mediated by family dynamics (Smokowski et al. 2009). Therefore, when working clinically with Southeast Asian youth, it is recommended to assess the levels of acculturation of the whole family, as differences in acculturation between youth and their parents have been shown to exist and may potentially contribute to familial stress and exacerbate violence in the home. Furthermore, supportive family dynamics have been cited as one of the most important protective factors against many youth problems and should be emphasized when working with Southeast Asian families.

References

Berry, J. W. (2001). A psychology of immigration. *Journal of Social Issues, 57,* 615–631. doi:10.1111/0022-4537.00231.

Brady, R. P. (2007, June). Psychometric characteristics and clinical use of the Youth Risk and Resilience Inventory (YRRI). Poster session abstract presented at the *2nd Annual Orthopsychiatric Summer Symposium of the American Orthopsychiatric Association.*

Castro, F. G., Garfinkle, J., Naranjo, D., Rollins, M., Book, J. S., & Book, D. W. (2007). Cultural traditions as "protective factors" among Latino children of illicit drug users. *Substance Use and Misuse, 42,* 621–642. doi:10.1080/10826080701202247.

Chan, S. (2004). *Survivors: Cambodian refugees in the United States.* Chicago, IL: University of Illinois Press.

Chung, R. C., Bemak, F., & Wong, S. (2000). Vietnamese refugees' levels of distress, social support, and acculturation: Implications for mental health counseling. *Journal of Mental Health Counseling, 22,* 150–161.

Dinh, K. T., Weinstein, T. L., Kim, S. Y., & Ho, I. K. (2008). Acculturative and psychological predictors of academic-related outcomes among Cambodian American high school students. *Journal of Southeast Asian American Education & Advancement, 3,* 1–25.

Kramer, E. J., Kwong, K., Lee, E., & Chung, H. (2002). Cultural factors influencing the mental health of Asian Americans. *The Western Journal of Medicine, 176*(4), 227–231.

Martinez-Torteya, C., Bogat, G. A., von Eye, A., & Levendosky, A. A. (2009). Resilience among children exposed to domestic violence: The role of risk and protective factors. *Child Development, 80,* 562–577. doi:10.1111/j.14678624.2009.01279.x.

National Crime Victimization Survey. (2008). Criminal victimization. U.S. Department of Justice, Bureau of Justice Statistics. Retrieved from http://www.ojp.usdoj.gov/bjs/pub/pdf/cv07.pdf.

National Asian Women's Health Organization. (2002). *Silence, not an option!*. San Francisco: Author.
Nguyen, A.-M. D., & Benet-Martínez, V. (2007). Biculturalism unpacked: Components, individual differences, measurement, and outcomes. *Social and Personality Psychology Compass, 1,* 101–114. doi:10.1111/j.17519004.2007.00029.x.
Rossman, B. B. (2001). Longer term effects of children's exposure to domestic violence. In S. A. Graham-Bermann & J. L. Edleson (Eds.), *Domestic violence in the lives of children: The future of research, intervention, and social policy* (pp. 35–66). Washington, DC: American Psychological Association.
Rutter, M. (1987). Psychosocial resilience and protective mechanisms. *American Journal of Orthopsychiatry, 57,* 316–331. doi:10.1111/j.1939-0025.1987.tb03541.x.
Serafica, F. C. (1997). Psychopathology and resiliency in Asian American children and adolescents. *Applied Developmental Science, 1,* 145–155. doi:10.1207/s1532480xads0103_5.
Smokowski, P. R., David-Ferdon, C., & Stroupe, N. (2009). Acculturation and violence in minority adolescents: A review of empirical literature. *Journal of Primary Prevention, 30,* 215–263. doi:10.1007/s10935-009-0173-0.
Southeast Asia Resource Action Center [SARAC]. (2003). *Southeast Asian American Population.* Retrieved from http://www.searac.org/poptable.html. doi:10.1177/0020764008094429.
Sue, D. W., & Sue, D. (2008). *Counseling the culturally diverse: Theory and practice* (5th ed.). New York: Wiley.
Suinn, R. M. (2001). *Psychosocial measures for Asian Americans: Tools for practices and research.* Retrieved from http://www.columbia.edu/cu/ssw/projects/pmap/docs/suinn_slasia.pdf.
Vargas-Reighley, R. (2005). *Bicultural competence and academic resilience among immigrants.* New York, NY: LFB Scholarly Publishers.
Xiong, Z. B., Eliason, P. A., Detzner, D. F., & Cleveland, M. J. (2005). Southeast Asian immigrants' perceptions of good adolescents and good parents. *The Journal of Psychology: Interdisciplinary and Applied, 139,* 159–175. doi:10.3200/JRLP.139.2.159-175.
Yoshihama, M., & Dabby, C. (2015). Facts & stats report: Domestic violence in Asian Pacific Islander homes. *Asian & Pacific Islander Institute on Domestic Violence.* Retrieved from http://www.api-gbv.org/files/Facts.Stats-APIIDV-2015.pdf.

FSC
www.fsc.org
MIX
Papier | Fördert gute Waldnutzung
FSC® C083411

Kolibri 360 GmbH
Ferdinand-Jühlke-Straße 7
99095 Erfurt, Deutschland
produktsicherheit@kolibri360.de